Rumi
the Book
of Love

Translations and Commentary by

**Coleman Barks**

with John Moyne, Nevit Ergin, A. J. Arberry, Reynold Nicholson, and M. G. Gupta

# Rumi

# the Book of Love

## Poems of Ecstasy and Longing

HarperOne
*An Imprint of* HarperCollins*Publishers*

HarperOne



HarperCollins Web site: http://www.harpercollins.com



FIRST HARPERCOLLINS PAPERBACK EDITION PUBLISHED IN 2005

Library of Congress Cataloging-in-Publication Data
Jalal al-Din Rumi, Maulana, 1207–1273.
[Poems. English. Selections]
Rumi : the book of love : poems of ecstasy and longing / translations and commentary by Coleman Barks.
p. cm.
Includes bibliographical references and index.
ISBN 978–0–06–302577–6

RELIGION / SPIRITUALITY

1. Jalål al-Dån Råmå, Maulana, 1207–1273—Translations into English. I. Title: Book of love. II. Barks, Coleman. III. Title.

PK6480.E5 B362 2002
891'.5511—dc21

2002032700

2 4 6 8 10 9 7 5 3 1

Printed and bound in India by Thomson Press India Ltd

MIX
Paper
FSC FSC® C010615

This book is produced from independently certified FSC® paper to ensure responsible forest management.

for Judith Orloff

# Contents

# Preface

I have sold too many books. Rumi translations have no business cresting in a wave of over half a million. It's like selling picnic tickets to an unmarked minefield. You wouldn't expect there to be a rush, but somehow there is. I may have left out something big and basic, like lowercase *islam* (submission). This love poetry is meant to obliterate you lovers. Rumi wants us to *surrender.* I bow to the grandeur of his full prostration. I never want to diminish that. This is not Norman Vincent Peale urging cheerfulness, conventional morality, and soft-focus, white-light feel-good, nor is this New Age tantric energy exchange. This is giving your life to the one within that you know as *Lord,* which is a totally private matter. No one except you can judge how that is going. But if you're not doing it, Rumi says, you are wasting your time here. Where's the solace of that statement? I once told a greeting card company that wanted to put Rumi verses on a card, "Rumi's poetry wants to dissolve the lovers. Annihilation is the point." There was a long silence on the other end. "Is there a holiday?"

Maybe we're ripe for Rumi's knowing, his way of love. I hope so. I take great delight in meeting bright twelve-year-olds who love certain Rumi poems, such as "The Guest House." They know the media and their community have lied to them about love, with all the fake love stories. They hear Rumi trying to tell them some truth about love, and they appreciate it. Maybe it's time to hear about going-in, about the joy of the witness in love, in meditation, in dreams, time to meet the one who looks into the creek.

Maybe we long now for the silence he loves. Say we're tiny blind cavefish swimming a gorgeous dark. We love the mountain the cave is inside, and somehow we love the sun, even though we haven't seen it and maybe never will. *That's* the love these poems sing, so how come they're wildly popular? I don't know.

In Marina del Rey, a posh southern California beach community, there's a side of a building painted shades of blue, on the left where Washington meets the beach. It has a Rumi quote high up in the right-hand corner. The ground floors of the beachside condos are garages stacked with Corvettes and Lexi and Jaguars, mostly shiny black, Bentleys, old BMW convertibles, fancy Lincoln off-road vehicles, and custom cars with no brand name. Upstairs among the Chinese objets and the Edwardian sideboards and the Motherwells, more often than not you will find on the thick glass, stylishly low, bedside table a well-read copy of *The Essential Rumi*.

A creative writing teacher on the prime-time show *Judging Amy* holds up two books, *The Great Gatsby* and *The Essential Rumi*, "Read these and learn how to write." Alec Baldwin has the book briefly in his hand in a movie whose title I can't recall. That book has achieved the cultural status of an empty Diet Coke can! It's everywhere. It's recommended summer reading in a two-page newsletter put out by a women's clothing store, Kathleen Sommers of San Antonio.

Philip Glass goes on world tour with *Monsters of Grace*, a choral piece using Rumi's words. Donna Karan reads Rumi on the fashion runway showing her new line. Madonna and Demi Moore read his poems on a Deepak CD. What to make of Rumi-mania? *This too shall pass?* Of course it will. For the first twenty years of the last century, I have heard, the most read book of poetry was Fitzgerald's *Rubaiyat of*

*Omar Khayyam,* far and away. No one reads that much now but graduate students.

I remember standing in the Intimate Bookstore in Chapel Hill in the late 1950s reading Walter Bennett's *This Is My Beloved,* a gift book of love poetry that every now and then mentions pubic hair, as I recall. There were other lightweights in the same area. I thought of them as books people bought and gave each other but never actually read. The packaging implied something sweet and romantic inside. There were Japanese haiku collections and very skinny pastel Emily Dickinsons on that shelf too, which is a violation of the Truth in Labeling Act. She and Basho are not easy company. Rod McKuen was nearby. The poetry community, with good reason, sees popularity as suspect. Billy Collins is having to fight that, a little. Maya Angelou has signed on with Hallmark.

But *Idylls of the King* my foot, I am more serious about living, and was even in the 1950s. I never bought books from the candy shelf. I gave my sexy Russian-Jewish college sweetheart a big collection of e. e. cummings. In the *slipshod mucus etcetera,* we were undergraduates who started a magazine whose first issue got banned by the Honor Council, and I had published a very strange Wolfean short story in the *Carolina Quarterly.* In my button-down I was deep into Colin Wilson and the mystics mentioned in *The Outsider.* Hesse, Boehme, Eckhart. I had Evelyn Underhill's *Mysticism* by my garret bed, and I told people I wanted to teach a course in mysticism. There were no mysticism courses at any college I ever went to, Berkeley and North Carolina.

Let's say there are two shelves, one with the true mystics and at the front of the store, the fad love-books. I want this on the former, please. Jelaluddin Rumi and Shamsi Tabriz are real. They gave the human condition one of the best shots it's been given. Rumi's poetry records that

Friendship, and that accounts for its wide appeal. Forget the movie stars. I met a guy behind the counter at West Building Supply in Athens, Georgia, who asked deep questions about the *Delicious Laughter* collection. "What's this with Eyes Shut Facing Eyes Wide Open?" Sit down with him. It may be this book will make it to the front of the store for Valentine's, but it's too rebellious to be there. It will not really behave itself anywhere in the store, not on the Islamic shelf, not in the poetry section, although maybe with the cookbooks. It likes cookbooks.

Alice Munro has a collection of stories called *Hateship, Friendship, Courtship, Loveship, Marriage.* I've not read it, but I might. I like to watch the changing moods and nuances of falling in and out of love, and so does Rumi. He's not some mystic snob. He sees the beauty and importance of anything human beings do, no matter how scandalous or violent. The slipping and sliding around sex, the posturing of combatants prior to combat. But he always uses human incident as a lens to look into soul growth. The idea of *commitment,* that staple of psychology, doesn't come up, nor any *fear of intimacy* scolding, no *shoulds* and *oughts.*

> It doesn't matter that you've broken your vow
> a thousand times. Still come,
> and yet again, come.

Rumi was an enlightened lover, a true human being, realized, whatever you want to call those who get to be deeply themselves. I had a dream once where I felt the grace of a continuing connection with my teacher, Bawa Muhaiyaddeen, who told me to do this Rumi work. Bawa was also a true human being. The transmission from him in me was, in the dream, visible in my eyes and also apparent in the currency, the popularity, of Rumi's poetry. My advice with this book, then, is to try, as he says, to listen for the *presences inside poems.* Connect there with an open heart, and follow the oceanfrog if he starts for home.[1]

I have been lucky (I guess) not to have to write for a living. I taught school, and now the retirement and the social security are enough. That's not to say I don't cash the Rumi royalty checks and go on NPR to talk about poetry. I do. But the fame and fortune numbers don't motivate me. I wait for the next poem. That keeps me going, what Robert Bly calls the honey of words. The taste and the taste again. Though that sounds a little too pure. I want recognition and reward as much as anyone.

And to be absolutely clear, neither this book nor its title was my idea. My editors at Harper San Francisco, and my agent, suggested the project. But as I've gotten into putting it together, I have made the book mine, perhaps to their chagrin. I'm not positive, but I'll bet they expected more of a lean toward flowers than toward annihilation. There are flowers here certainly. The sweetness in much of Rumi is undeniable. Anyway, your editorial instincts were right, and I'm very grateful, Steve, Kris, John, Eric, Kathi, Reid.

I once calculated that Rumi books sell at least a hundred a day right through weekends and holidays, while my own writing goes at about twelve copies a month, worldwide. Those numbers keep me humble. I am just about the humblest person one could ever meet. And I do look at the dotcom numbers. Maybe it's true to say that this writing is for fortune and fame *as well as* the pouring forth of vision and revision. Oh, what is so tiresome and fatuous as a mystic poet talking sales and mixed motivation? I do not know. Where is Jim Dickey when we need him. But listen. I have thought of a wisdom.

THIS IS THE MATERIAL PLANE

AND EVERY OUTWARD THING WE DO IS INNER WORK

Sew that on a sampler and hang it in the kitchen. Or,

THIS IS THE MATERIAL PLANE
AND IT COULD USE A GOOD SANDING

Poetry and music are two great mysteries of human consciousness. Rumi lets them pour through as a beauty we are, and a kind of a home too.

COLEMAN BARKS
*Athens, GA*
*July 18, 2002*

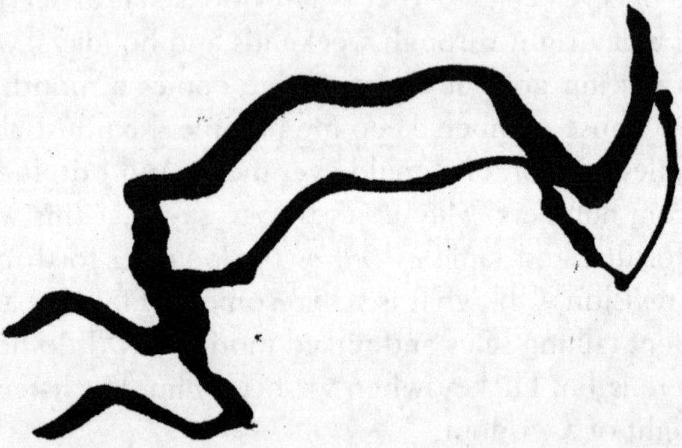

# *Introduction:*
# *The Magnificent Regions of the Heart*

In certain places and times the current of mystical awareness runs deep and strong, more so than in others. Among the Greeks in the sixth century B.C. and also in India and China during that century. Jesus and the desert fathers. The Hassidic masters in Poland and Russia in the seventeenth and eighteenth centuries and the Zen masters in Japan during the same period were also part of an inexplicable flooding.

In the Persian empire from the eleventh to the fourteenth century a brilliant flowering of awareness came among the Sufis, and especially the poets. Jelaluddin Rumi (1207–1273) was one of those conductors of knowing and being. Sufis call Rumi the *Qutb,* the pole, of love. Gilani (d. 1166) was the pole of power and Ibn Arabi (1165–1249), of knowledge. Through Rumi comes a transmission of the divine to this planet in the regions of love. His poetry is a record of his enduring the experience of living at the core. In each human being there is a meeting with the divine. That intersection is the heart.

Sometimes we sense that love is our expertise, despite the obviously murderous bent of these days and hours. Still, we do love in many different ways. Let me count them. There are as many ways of loving as there are people, and that wildflower variety is the great beauty of this dimension of existence. I had a dream once where I saw a blue tinge to everything, and I knew, I felt, how the blueness was love. We couldn't see it with ordinary vision, but for dream-seeing it was there, drenching the planet, which does appear blue, as we know, from space.

At poetry readings I have said about Rumi's poetry, "Folks, this is not country music." It gets a laugh. Rumi says, Fall in love in such a way that it frees you from any connecting. That's very different from the lonely wail of: She left me, he left me; she came back; she left again. Some of his lines have been put in songs. There is a grief of separation in them, but the words come from a different region than popular lyrics. I'm not saying there's not wisdom in country songs. There is plenty. The love that Rumi and Shams move into, though, includes those dimensions and moves through them to what Sufis call the *qalb*. I have no synonym for that, and perhaps not much experience of it, though I met one who lives there, Bawa Muhaiyaddeen. I am no great sheikhs of a lover myself. I get mean and jealous, distracted and forgetful. It's Rumi's and Bawa's station I try to speak of, not mine. At the end of his life Ouspensky told J. G. Bennett in a letter that nothing could be found by intellectual processes, and that "there is only one hope: that we should find a way to work with the higher emotional centre." That is the work that Rumi's poetry is about.

Sufis say the heart is "the comprehensive human reality,"[2] and that the way of love is a path of annihilation, of the beatitude of "as though it had never been." Our original state is nonbeing, nonexistence, and we spend much of our lives trying to break free of matter, free of mind and desire, back into the deep region of being and nonbeing we are at the core. The refreshment of dreamless sleep when we are, but are not conscious, is a taste of it. We are here, then, but with no awareness of being here.

The absolute ipseity, suchness, the human reality and not the melodrama, that region of being, is described in the Heart Sutra, the central text of Zen, as having "no eyes, no ears, no nose, no tongue, no body, no mind, and no consciousness."[3] To get there you must die before you die. Buddha's Heart Sutra draws one along to the understanding that in that dissolving nothing exists by itself. Everything interpenetrates in the ecstatic core where heart-vision begins.

A bowl falls from the roof. This is not theoretical. It is the practical and experiential love that annihilates, and the most ineffable of experiences, if there can be degrees of unsayableness. All of Rumi's poems may be heard as love poems. They attend the soul's flowering from grief, and from every emotion that streams through the guest house of consciousness.

The love way is not religious. It is rather the origin and the longing inside religiousness. Footprints disappear at the ocean's edge. When we bow to each other, feet become head in a circle. No one could tell with Rumi and Shams who was teacher and who the student. Lover, beloved, and love became one thing with them. Images of transparency and particles, light upon light, the candle at noon, occur, images of breath merging with sky. We are sleeping and wake inside another sleep; we wake again, and on . . . as veils, the mist of language, the apparent limits, burn off. Each region of love leads to the unfolding. There may seem to be a kind of progress to this book, from spontaneous wandering to the lord of the heart, but it might just as easily be reversed, or put in any number of sequences. The heart with its many regions moves more like interpenetrating spheres, concurrent universes, than a linear path. Areas of energy in the poetry merge with one another as layers of ocean, or as the mysterious workings of soil in a field, or the draining slant of a mountainside.

Rumi's impulse feels earthward in its transformation, going down instead of up in the way one might aspire to the angelic. There is no down or up in love, but if one had to say whether Rumi's poetry goes more with the pure transcenders or more with the grief-gardeners, one would say he's a ground-hugger and not so much a high-flyer, more *jamal* (feminine, receptive) than *jalal* (masculine, commanding). But as Rumi himself says hundreds of times, there is little one can *say* about love. It has to be lived, and it's always in motion.

When Rainer Maria Rilke, the great mystical poet of the twentieth century, saw the Mevlevi dervishes in Cairo in 1910, he said, "With Rumi the scale is shifted, for this is the mystery of the deeply kneeling man. In following the peculiar weight and strength in his knees, he belongs to that world in which height is depth. This is the night of radiant depth unfolded." He was referring to the night of December 17, when Rumi died in 1273. It is celebrated as his union with the divine.

# *A Brief Account of Rumi's Life*

Rumi was born in Balkh, a small town west of Mazar-i-Sharif in Afghanistan on September 30, 1207. Fleeing the approach of Genghis Khan's Mongol armies, the family moved several times, to Waksh in what is now Tajikistan, to Samarkand, to Damascus, finally settling in Konya on the high plain of central Anatolia. Rumi's father, Bahauddin, was a highly original mystic who kept his intimations of, and promptings from, the divine in diary form. The *Ma'arif* was one of Rumi's most treasured texts after Bahauddin's death. He studied it with his father's former student, Burhanuddin Mahaqqiq. They also read Sanai and Attar together, and Burhan led the young Rumi on several consecutive *chillas*, forty-day fasting retreats. Burhan was himself an eccentric hermit majestically unconcerned with beliefs and lineages. He seems to have prepared Jelaluddin well for the galvanizing event of the young mystic's life, his meeting with Shamsi Tabriz.

In late October of 1244 Rumi was thirty-seven. Shams was twenty, maybe thirty, years older. Their meeting and subsequent *sohbet* (mystical conversation) generated fresh stories and ecstatic icons for the world of mystical awareness and love. Their Friendship is one of the great mysteries. Rumi's poetry is heard as continuing resonance from That. Their separation on the physical plane occurred four years later on December 5, 1248. There is disagreement now as to how Shams disappeared. Franklin Lewis claims that the rumor Shams was murdered by jealous disciples of Rumi "arrives late, circulates in oral context, and is almost certainly groundless."[4] What we know for sure is what we have, the poems so filled with grief and ecstatic sentience. All the biographical scenarios, whichever one chooses, are without sufficient evidence to be authoritative. No matter. We can let that detective story rest awhile. We have the *Shams,* the *Masnavi,* the letters, Discourses, sermons, the *Rubaiyat,* a generous plenty!

After Shams's death or disappearance, Rumi lived twenty-six years tending soul growth in the dervish community around him and leaving us a prodigious legacy. He spoke the poetry spontaneously. It was taken down by scribes, and he revised it later in manuscript. Rumi was married twice; his first wife, Gowhar Khatun, died young. She bore two children, Sultan Velad and Allaedin. Rumi had two children also with his second wife, Kira Khatun: Mozaffer, a son, and Maleke, a daughter.

The central enigma of Rumi's life, of course, is Shams Tabriz, the electrifying, eccentric wanderer with the charisma of a desert wind, who knelt and prayed for a companion on his own level of attainment. A voice came, *What will you give?* "My head." *Jelaluddin of Konya is your Friend.* He said later that he came to Rumi when Rumi was ready to receive his secret. But it was observed of Rumi and Shams that one could not tell who was the teacher and who the disciple.

Thoreau went to the woods to simplify and find what was most deeply his. "I did not want to live what was not life. Living is so dear." Some sentences sear the soul free of communal and personal habits, the situation we're born within. When Shams pushes Rumi's books into the fountain at their first meeting, including his father Bahauddin's soul notes, he says, "Now you must live what you've been reading and talking about."

Rumi relinquishes his books, and he and Shams go into retreat. Rumi asks for burning. Shams says, I am fire. It is that which refines the poems to their daring intensity and courage, to their setting out into unknown regions, these heart-quadrants that are so subtle and multivalent.

Why should I seek more?
I am the same as he.

His essence speaks through me.
I have been looking for myself.

After this soul-merging with Shams, Rumi found another living friend with whom to do the heart-opening work, Saladin Zarkub the goldsmith. Saladin was an old man (the poems become more quiet and tender), and after Saladin's death, Husam Chelebi, Rumi's scribe, became the friend of his heart. They produced the six books of the *Masnavi*. Rumi died as the sky turned deep red at sunset on December 17, 1273. There were minor tremors, like stomach grumblings. "Patience, old earth!" Rumi called out. "You'll have your sweet morsel soon!"

# Rumi
# the Book of Love

# 1. *Spontaneous Wandering*

I take down my King James to look up the passage about love (charity) in 1 Corinthians 13. There is a tiny red ant living in Corinth. It walks to the top and along the gold edges. Spontaneous wandering is a favorite region of the heart. It may look like mindless drift, but it isn't. More the good Don and Sancho out for their inspired adventures, quixotic and panzaic.[5] The ant is my teacher.

We see through a glass darkly, then face-to-face. A more polished mirror shows us who we truly are. The wandering of Rumi's poetry is a model for the soul's lovely motions. When thirst begins to look for water, water has already started out with a canteen, looking for thirst. Love feels like sliding along the eddies and currents of the tao.

Pir Vilayat Khan[6] recently commented to me, "Your first Rumi volumes seemed very sexual." He's right. There is too much of that energy in the first work with Rumi I did, especially in some of the quatrains. I was very wet with such water at the time myself. I was thirty-nine. Now I'm sixty-five. Things change; nothing wrong with that. What's truly alive is always changing.

Gay lovers hear Rumi's poetry as gay. I don't agree, though I'm certainly guilty of previously loading Rumi's poetry with erotic fruit. I don't do that now. Rumi is way happier than sex and orgasms, his wandering more conscious and free. See "Imra'u 'l-Qays" in the next section. Rumi and Shams wander in that country.

Perhaps the purest wanderer of our time is Nanao, like Basho in his. Gary Snyder says about him,

> This subtropical East China Sea carpenter and spear fisherman finds himself equally at home in the desert. So much so that on one occasion when an eminent traditional Buddhist priest boasted of his lineage, Nanao responded, "I need no lineage. I am desert rat." But for all his independence Nanao Sakaki carries the karma of Chungtzu, En-no-gyoja, Saigyo, Ikkyu, Basho, and Issa in his bindle. His work or play in the world is to pull out nails, free seized nuts, break loose the rusted, open up the shutters. You can put these poems in your shoes and walk a thousand miles.

## GO WITH MUDDY FEET

When you hear dirty story
        wash your ears.
When you see ugly stuff
        wash your eyes.
When you get bad thoughts
        wash your mind.
                and
Keep your feet muddy.[7]

—Nanao Sakaki

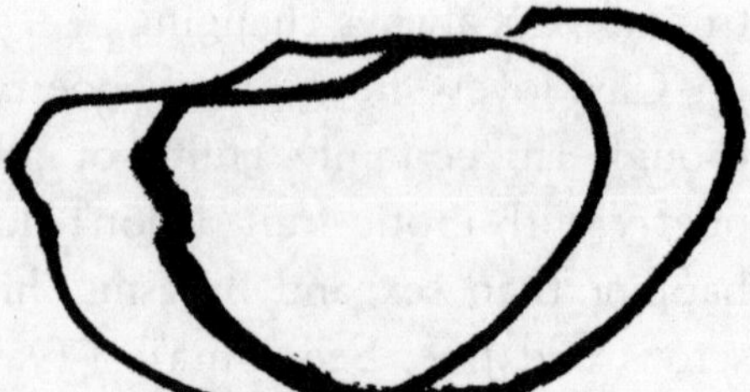

Excuse my wandering.
How can one be orderly with this?
It's like counting leaves in a garden,

along with the song notes of partridges,
and crows. Sometimes organization
and computation become absurd.

## FIVE THINGS

I have five things to say,
five fingers to give into your grace.

First, when I was apart from you,
this world did not exist, nor any other.

Second, whatever I was looking for
was always you.

Third, why did I ever learn to count to three?

Fourth, my cornfield is burning!

Fifth, this finger stands for Rabia,[8]
and this is for someone else.
Is there a difference?

Are these words or tears?
Is weeping speech?
What shall I do, my love?

So the lover speaks, and everyone around
begins to cry with him, laughing crazily,
moaning in the spreading union
of lover and beloved.

This is the true religion. All others
are thrown-away bandages beside it.

This is the *sema*[9] of slavery and mastery
dancing together. This is not-being.

I know these dancers.
Day and night I sing their songs
in this phenomenal cage.

## THE MANY WINES

God has given us a dark wine so potent that,
drinking it, we leave the two worlds.

God has put into the form of hashish a power
to deliver the taster from self-consciousness.

God has made sleep
so that it erases every thought.

God made Majnun love Layla so much
that just her dog would cause confusion in him.[10]

There are thousands of wines
that can take over our minds.

Don't think all ecstasies
are the same!

Jesus was lost in his love for God.
His donkey was drunk on barley.

Drink from the presence of saints,
not from those other jars.

Every object, every being,
is a jar full of delight.

Be a connoisseur,
and taste with caution.

Any wine will get you high.
Judge like a king, and choose the purest,

the ones unadulterated with fear,
or some urgency about "what's needed."

Drink the wine that moves you
as a camel moves when it's been untied,
and is just ambling about.

## COOKED HEADS

I have been given a glass
that has the fountain of the sun inside,

a Friend in both worlds, like the fragrance
of amber inside the fragrance of musk.

My soul-parrot gets excited with sweetness.
Wingbeats, a door opening in the sun.

You've seen the market where they sell
cooked heads: that's what this is,

a way of seeing beyond inner and outer.[11]
A donkey wanders the sign of Taurus.

Heroes do not stay lined up in ranks
for very long. I set out for Tabriz,

even though my boat is anchored here.

## WHERE YOU LOVE FROM

Look inside and find where a person
loves from. That's the reality,
not what they say.
Hypocrites

give attention to form, the right
and wrong ways of professing belief.
Grow instead in universal light.

When that revealed itself, God gave it
a thousand different names, the least
of those sweet-breathing names being,
*the one who is not in need of anyone.*

You've so distracted me,
your absence fans my love.
Don't ask how.

Then you come near.
"Do not . . ." I say, and
"Do not . . . ," you answer.

Don't ask why
this delights me.

In your light I learn how to love.
In your beauty, how to make poems.

You dance inside my chest
where no one sees you,

but sometimes I do,
and that sight becomes this art.

Drumsound rises on the air,
its throb, my heart.

A voice inside the beat says,
"I know you're tired,
but come, this is the way."

Are you jealous of the ocean's generosity?
Why would you refuse to give
this love to anyone?

Fish don't hold the sacred liquid in cups!
They swim the huge fluid freedom.

## THERE'S NOTHING AHEAD

Lovers think they're looking for each other,
but there's only one search: wandering
this world is wandering that,
both inside one
transparent sky. In here there is
no dogma and no heresy.

The miracle of Jesus is himself, not what he said
or did about the future. Forget the future.
I'd worship someone who could do that.

On the way you may want to look back, or not.
But if you can say, *There's nothing ahead,*
there will be nothing there.
                                        Stretch your arms
and take hold the cloth of your clothes
with both hands. The cure for pain is in the pain.
Good and bad are mixed. If you don't have both,
you don't belong with us.
                                  When one of us gets lost,
is not here, he must be inside us. There's no
place like that anywhere in the world.

# 2. Sohbet: *Who You Talking To?*

For Rumi the appearance of formal beauty comes as a *natural* response to being spoken to. The rose opens because it has heard something. The cypress grows strong and straight because a love-secret is being whispered. Elegance in language arrives in *response.* Before creation there was a question, "Am I not your lord?"[12] The simultaneous *YES!* that came is why we are here at all in the midst of three hundred billion galaxies.

I have a friend who, when she wants to know who I am seeing, who I am in love with, asks, *Who you talking to?* The exchange of deep friendship makes a fine entrance into love and trust, into the mysterious *action* that moves through the eyes, the voice, the heart.

Rumi wonders, *Can you see these escapees, the ones who have gotten free of their personalities and into the truer self?* He celebrates the freedom of those escapees, how their friendship dissolves into *everything:* what anybody says, whatever happens.

Emily Dickinson says, *I dwell in possibility, a fairer house than prose.* That region where her poetry grew is *sohbet.*

I dwell in possibility,
A fairer house than prose,
More numerous of windows,
Superior for doors.

Of chambers as the cedars,
Impregnable of eye.
And for an everlasting roof
The gambrels of the sky.

Of visitors, the fairest.
For occupation, this:
The spreading wide my narrow hands
To gather paradise.[13]

She's describing the opening air around Rumi and Shams, their retreat house full of sky and breath, and laughter with the *fairest visitors.* Love with no object, conversation with no subject, seeing with no image, light on light, pure possibility.

Rumi's love poems are not in the realm we're more familiar with, the earthy and sexual transcendence celebrated in the poetry of Keats and Whitman, Rexroth, Kinnell, Bly, Creeley, Jack Gilbert. Rumi's love is beyond the sexual pathway and, for that reason, maybe not so beautiful, to us. Rumi is less tranced and less sensual than, say, these lines from Rexroth's late afternoon love poem, "When We with Sappho":

Stop reading. Lean back. Give me your mouth.
Your grace is as beautiful as a sleep.

You move against me like a wave
That moves in sleep.
Your body spreads across my brain
Like a bird-filled summer;
Not like a body, not like a separate thing,
But like a nimbus that hovers
Over every other thing in all the world.[14]

Sufis say there are three ways of being with the mystery: prayer, then a step up from that, meditation, and a step up from that, conversation, the mystical exchange they call *sohbet*.

## RESPONSE TO YOUR QUESTION

Why ask about behavior when you are soul-essence,
and a way of seeing into presence!
Plus you're with us!
How could you worry?
You may as well free a few words from
your vocabulary.
*Why* and *how* and *impossible.* Open
the mouth-cage
and let those fly away.
We were all born by
accident, but still this wandering caravan
will make camp in perfection.

Forget the nonsense categories of *there* and *here,*
race, nation, religion,
starting point and destination.

You are soul, and you *are* love,
not a sprite or an angel or a human being!
You're a
*Godman-womanGod-manGod-Godwoman!*
No more questions now
as to what it is we're *doing* here.

If you want what visible reality can give,
you're an employee.

If you want the unseen world,
you're not living your truth.

Both wishes are foolish,
but you'll be forgiven for forgetting
that what you really want is
love's confusing joy.

## SPECIAL PLATES

Notice how each particle moves.
Notice how everyone has just arrived here
from a journey. Notice how each wants
a different food. Notice how
the stars vanish as the sun comes up,
and how all streams stream toward the ocean.

Look at the chefs preparing special plates
for everyone according to what they need.
Look at this cup that can hold the ocean.
Look at those who see the face. Look
through Shams's eyes into water
that is entirely jewels.

## YOU ARE NOT YOUR EYES

Those who have reached their arms
into emptiness are no longer concerned
with lies and truth, with mind and soul,

or which side of the bed they rose from.
If you are still struggling to understand,
you are not there. You offer your soul

to one who says, "Take it to the other
side." You're on neither side, yet
those who love you see you on one side

or the other. You say *Illa,* "only God,"
then your hungry eyes see you're in
"nothing," *La.*[15] You're an artist

who paints both with existence and non.
Shams could help you see who you are,
but remember, *You are not your eyes.*

## WHAT WAS SAID TO THE ROSE

What was said to the rose that made it open
was said to me here in my chest.

What was told the cypress that made it strong
and straight, what was whispered the jasmine

so it is what it is, whatever made sugarcane
sweet; whatever was said to the inhabitants

of the town of Chigil in Turkestan that makes
them so handsome, whatever lets the pomegranate

flower blush like a human face, that is being
said to me now. I blush. Whatever put eloquence

in language, that's happening here. The great
warehouse doors open; I fill with gratitude,

chewing a piece of sugarcane, in love with
the one to whom every *that* belongs!

## THE MUSIC

For sixty years I have been forgetful,
every moment, but not for a second
has this flowing toward me slowed or stopped.
I deserve nothing. Today I recognize
that I am the guest the mystics talk about.
I play this living music for my host.
Everything today is for the host.

Imra'u 'l-Qays,[16] king of the Arabs,
was very handsome and a poet full of love songs.

Women loved him desperately. Everyone loved him,
but there came one night an experience
that changed him completely.

He left his kingdom and his family.
He put on dervish robes and wandered
from one weather, one landscape, to another.

Love dissolved his king-self and led him to Tabuk,
where he worked for a time making bricks.

Someone told the king of Tabuk about Imra'u 'l-Qays,
and that king came to visit him at night.

"King of the Arabs, handsome Joseph of this age,
ruler of two empires, one composed of territories,
and the other of the beauty of women,

if you would consent to stay with me,
I would be honored. You abandon kingdoms,
because you want more than kingdoms."

The king of Tabuk went on like this, praising
Imra'u 'l-Qays and talking theology and philosophy.

Imra'u 'l-Qays kept silent.
Then suddenly he leaned and whispered something
in the second king's ear, and that second
king became a wild wanderer too.

They walked out of town hand in hand,
no royal belts, no thrones.

This is what love does and continues to do.
It tastes like honey to adults and milk to children.

Love is the last thirty-pound bale.
When you load it on, the boat tips over.

So they wandered around China like birds
pecking at bits of grain. They rarely spoke
because of the dangerous seriousness
of the secret they knew.

That love-secret spoken pleasantly, or irritation,
severs a hundred thousand heads in one swing.

A love-lion grazes in the soul's pasture,
while the scimitar of this secret approaches.
It's a killing better than any living.

All that world-power wants, really,
is this weakness.

So these kings talk in low tones,
and carefully. Only God knows what they say.

They use unsayable words. Bird language.
But some people have imitated them, learned
a few birdcalls, and gotten prestigious.

# 3. *The Superabundance of Ordinary Being*

Love is not love that doesn't love the details of the beloved, the minute particulars. Judith and I were in Pammukkalle, Turkey, an ancient Roman bath with a museum, and around the side, attached to it, is a shed called the Museum of Small Findings. Shards of pottery, coins, fingers and toes of statuary, just as the sign says. The guard at the door, the host, is a smiling, genial man about four-feet two-inches tall, no taller, and no pun intended. Wherever we go now we do *small findings,* to make sure nothing goes unnoticed, or gets left behind.

Love is the connection with spirit, and one way it flows is through form. That's the state of rapture Rumi praises, the joy of being inside an intersection with the divine, which is what this world is.

"Truly being here is glorious," says Rilke in the *Seventh Duino Elegy,* and in the *Ninth,*

> Isn't it the secret intent
> of this taciturn earth, when it forces lovers together,
> that inside their boundless emotion all things may
> shudder with joy?

This resonant trembling of the earth with lovers, is the *superabundance* of *being,* a phrase from Rilke in Stephen Mitchell's translation.[17]

Rumi walks the granary amazed like an ant, small findings the given.

## ZULEIKHA

Zuleikha[18] let everything be the name of Joseph,
from celery seed to aloes wood. She loved him
so much she concealed his name in many phrases,
the inner meanings known only to her.
When she said,
*The wax is softening near the fire,* she meant,
*My love is wanting me.*
If she said, *Look, the moon is up,*
or *The willow has new leaves,* or *The coriander seeds*
*have caught fire,* or *The king is in a good mood today,*
or *Isn't that lucky,* or *The furniture needs dusting,* or
*The water carrier is here,* or *This bread needs more salt,*
or *The clouds seem to be moving against the wind,*
or *My head hurts,* or *My headache's better,*
anything she praises it's Joseph's touch she means.
Any complaint, it's his being away.

When she's hungry, it's for him. Thirsty, his name
is a sherbet. Cold, he's a fur. This is what
the Friend can do when one is in such love.

The miracle Jesus did by being the name of God,
Zuleikha felt in the name Joseph.

When one is united to the core of another,
to speak of that is to breathe the name *Hu*,
empty of self and filled with love.

## PUT THIS DESIGN IN YOUR CARPET

Spiritual experience is a modest woman
who looks lovingly at one man.

It's a great river where ducks live
happily, and crows drown. The visible

bowl of form contains food that is both
nourishing and a source of heartburn.

There is an unseen presence we honor
that gives the gifts.

You're water. We're the millstone.
You're wind. We're dust blown up into shapes.

You're spirit. We're the opening and closing
of our hands. You're the clarity.

We're this language that tries to say it.
You're joy. We're all the different kinds

of laughing. Any movement or sound
is a profession of faith, as the millstone

grinding is explaining how it believes
in the river! No metaphor can say this,

but I can't stop pointing to the beauty.
Every moment and place says,

"Put this design in your carpet!"

## THE ROAD HOME

An ant hurries along a threshing floor
with its wheat grain, moving between huge stacks
of wheat, not knowing the abundance
all around. It thinks its one grain
is all there is to love.

So we choose a tiny seed to be devoted to.
This body, one path or one teacher.
Look wider and farther.

The essence of every human being can see,
and what that essence-eye takes in,
the being becomes. Saturn. Solomon!

The ocean pours through a jar,
and you might say it swims inside
the fish! This mystery gives peace to
your longing and makes the road home home.

## THIS IS ENOUGH

Aphrodite singing *ghazals*. A sky with
gold streaks across. A stick

that finds water in stone. Jesus
sitting quietly near the animals.

Night so peaceful. *This is enough*
was always true. We just haven't

seen it. The hoopoe already wears
a tufted crown. Each ant is given

its elegant belt at birth. This love
we feel pours through us like a giveaway

song. The source of *now* is here!

## UZAYR

Which reminds me of the sons of Uzayr,
who are out looking for their father.

They have grown old, and their father
has miraculously grown young!

They meet him and ask, "Pardon us, sir,
but have you seen Uzayr? We hear

that he's supposed to be coming along
this road today." "Yes," says Uzayr,

"he's right behind me." One of his sons
replies, "That's good news." The other

falls on the ground. He has recognized
his father. "What do you mean news?

We're already inside the sweetness
of his presence." To the mind

there is such a thing as news, whereas
to inner knowing, it's all in the middle

of its happening. To doubters, this is
a pain. To believers, it's gospel.

To the lover and the visionary,
it's life as it's being lived.

Out of nowhere a horse
brought us here where we taste love
until we don't exist again. This taste
is the wine we always mention.

## AMAZED MOUTH

The soul: a wide listening sky
with thousands of candles.

When anything is sold, soul gets given
in the cash: people waiting at a door,

a ladder leaning on a roof, someone
climbing down. The market square bright

with understanding. Listening
opens its amazed mouth.

Birdsong, wind,
the water's face.

Each flower, remembering the smell:
I know you're close by.

## BEGIN

This is now. Now is. Don't postpone
till then. Spend the spark of iron

on stone. Sit at the head of the table.
Dip your spoon in the bowl. Seat yourself

next to your joy and have your awakened soul
pour wine. Branches in the spring wind,

easy dance of jasmine and cypress. Cloth
for green robes has been cut from pure

absence. You're the tailor, settled
among his shop goods, quietly sewing.

# 4. *Sudden Wholeness*

In this love kingdom there's a windy blowing open of windows. Spring! Sounds of talking sprout. There's a picnic by the river. Identity is music, and poems are rough notations of the melodies.

This station gives the lover glimpses of a spirit-wholeness running through the apparent chaos, a rightness that weaves a pattern the lover sees in the dissonant and daily.

Here is the auspicious beginning. Kindness stands in the door. You walk out together like the Zen master Basho moving around Kyoto, pining for Kyoto. The phenomenal and the numinous grow identical. The world you see, together with the poem, both are intensely alive inside each other with revelation and suchness. That's the feeling in this region: continuous seasonal epiphany, grief, elation, whimsy.

Samurai talk —
tang
of horse radish.

You, the butterfly —
I, Chuang Tzu's
dreaming heart.

Even in Kyoto —
hearing the cuckoo's cry —
I long for Kyoto.[19]

## THIS MARKET

Can you find another market like this?
Where, with your one rose

you can buy hundreds of rose gardens?
Where, for one seed you get

a whole wilderness? For one weak
breath, the divine wind?

## THE MUSIC WE ARE

Did you hear that winter's over?
The basil and the carnations

cannot control their laughter.
The nightingale, back from his wandering,

has been made singing master over
all the birds. The trees reach out

their congratulations. The soul
goes dancing through the king's doorway.

Anemones blush because they have seen
the rose naked. Spring, the only fair

judge, walks in the courtroom, and
several December thieves steal away.

Last year's miracles will soon be
forgotten. New creatures whirl in

from nonexistence, galaxies scattered
around their feet. Have you met them?

Do you hear the bud of Jesus crooning
in the cradle? A single narcissus

flower has been appointed Inspector
of Kingdoms. A feast is set. Listen.

The wind is pouring wine! Love
used to hide inside images. No more!

The orchard hangs out its lanterns.
The dead come stumbling by in shrouds.

Nothing can stay bound or be imprisoned.
You say, "End this poem here and

wait for what's next." I will. Poems
are rough notations for the music we are.

## WALNUTS

Philosophers have said that we love music
because it resembles the sphere-sounds

of union. We've been part of a harmony
before, so these moments of treble and bass

keep our remembering fresh. But how
does this happen within these dense bodies

full of forgetfulness and doubt and
grieving? It's like water passing through us.

It becomes acidic and bitter, but still as
urine it retains watery qualities.

It will put out a fire! So there is this music
flowing through our bodies that can dowse

restlessness. Hearing the sound, we gather
strength. Love kindles with melody. Music

feeds a lover composure, and provides form
for the imagination. Music breathes

on personal fire and makes it keener.
The waterhole is deep. A thirsty man climbs

a walnut tree growing next to the pool
and drops walnuts one by one into

the beautiful place. He listens carefully
to the sound as they hit and watches

the bubbles. A more rational man gives advice,
"You'll regret doing this. You're so far

from the water that by the time you get down
to gather walnuts, the water will have

carried them away." He replies, "I'm not
here for walnuts, I want the music

they make when they hit."

You that come to birth and bring the mysteries,
your voice-thunder makes us very happy.

Roar, lion of the heart,
and tear me open!

## NO BETTER GIFT

When the ocean comes to you as a lover,
marry, at once, quickly,
for God's sake!

Don't postpone it!
Existence has no better gift.

No amount of searching
will find this.

A perfect falcon, for no reason,
has landed on your shoulder,
and become yours.

This moment this love comes to rest in me,
many beings in one being.
In one wheat grain a thousand sheaf stacks.
Inside the needle's eye, a turning night of stars.

The clear bead at the center changes everything.
There are no edges to my loving now.

You've heard it said there's a window
that opens from one mind to another,

but if there's no wall, there's no need
for fitting the window, or the latch.

A thousand half-loves
must be forsaken to take
one whole heart home.

## PATTERN

When love itself comes to kiss you,
don't hold back! When the king goes hunting,

the forest smiles. Now the king has become
the place and all the players, prey,

bystander, bow, arrow, hand and release.
How does *that* feel? Last night's dream

enters these open eyes. We sometimes make
spiderwebs of smoke and saliva, fragile

thought-packets. Leave thinking to the one
who gave intelligence. Stop weaving,

and watch how the pattern improves.

## AUCTION

As elephants remember India
perfectly, as mind dissolves,
as song begins, as the glass
fills, wind rising, a roomful
of conversation, a sanctuary
of prostration, a bird lights
on my hand in this day born
of friends, an ocean covering
everything, all roads opening,
a person changing to kindness,
no one reasonable, religious
jargon forgotten, and Saladin
there raising his hand to bid
on the bedraggled boy Joseph!

# 5. *Escaping into Silence*

Close the language-door (the mouth). Open the love-window (the eyes). The moon (the reflected light of the divine) won't use the door, only the window. Moving into silence with a friend, and with what comes through the eyes and both presences then, we may become those escapees Rumi calls *those who associate in the heart.*

Rumi celebrates this wild freedom, and as he does, he may seem to be subverting scripture with his advocacy of the nonverbal, but he's actually trying to make the revelation that comes in language more experiential. I recommend we all try a day of silence with someone. Just one day!

## QUIETNESS

Inside this new love, die.
Your way begins on the other side.
Become the sky.
Take an ax to the prison wall.
Escape. Walk out
like someone suddenly born into color.
Do it now.
You're covered with thick cloud.
Slide out the side. Die,
and be quiet. Quietness is the surest
sign that you've died.
Your old life was a frantic running
from silence.

The speechless full moon comes out now.

## SOME KISS WE WANT

There is some kiss we want
with our whole lives, the touch

of spirit on the body. Seawater
begs the pearl to break its shell.

And the lily, how passionately
it needs some wild darling!

At night, I open the window and ask
the moon to come and press its
face against mine.

Breathe into me. Close
the language-door and open the love-window.
The moon won't use the door,
only the window.

## THE WATERWHEEL

Stay together, friends.
Don't scatter and sleep.

Our friendship is made
of being awake.

The waterwheel accepts water
and turns and gives it away,
weeping.

That way it stays in the garden,
whereas another roundness rolls
through a dry riverbed looking
for what it thinks it wants.

Stay here, quivering with each moment
like a drop of mercury.

## BLESSING THE MARRIAGE

This marriage be wine with halvah,
honey dissolving in milk.

This marriage be the leaves and fruit
of a date tree. This marriage

be women laughing together for days
on end. This marriage, a sign

for us to study. This marriage,
beauty. This marriage, a moon

in a light blue sky. This marriage,
this silence, fully mixed with spirit.

## TWO DAYS OF SILENCE

After days of feasting, fast.
After days of sleeping, stay awake
one night. After these times of bitter
storytelling, joking, and serious
considerations, we should give ourselves
two days between layers of baklava
in the quiet seclusion where soul sweetens
and thrives more than with language.

I hear nothing in my ear but your voice.
Heart has plundered mind of its eloquence.

Love writes a transparent calligraphy, so on
the empty page my soul can read and recollect.

Which is worth more, a crowd of thousands,
or your own genuine solitude?
Freedom, or power over an entire nation?

A little while alone in your room
will prove more valuable than anything else
that could ever be given you.

## PASSAGE INTO SILENCE

The essence of darkness is light,
as oil is the essence of this light.

You are the origin of all jasmine, narcissi,
and irises to come.
You are sunlight moving
through the houses, David's hand
molding smooth chainmail,
September moon
over the unharvested crop. You *set*
the grain in the husk.
A rose torn open, my head
not worrying about debt, you,
soul and body
mortared together in bed,
you saying,
*you are, you are,*
then stopping to twist the strings
to sweeten the voice.
When I give this body
to the ground, you will find
another way.
These words are an alternate
existence. Hear the passage into
silence and be that.

# 6. *A New Life*

As one becomes a lover, duties change to inspirations. Practices become dance, poetry, creek music moving along. Impossible natural images of transformation appear: candle becomes moth; a dry, broken stick breaks into bud. A chickpea becomes its cook (not so impossible, the natural tasting!). Something enters that spontaneously enjoys itself. Finding a purpose for acting is no longer the problem. The soul is here for its own joy. Eyes are meant to see things. It's by some grand shift of energy that we know love.

We have this great love-ache for the ocean and the seabirds sewing the hem of her robe. That is the subject here. We long for beauty, even as we swim within it. Abdul Qadir Gilani describes this region of the heart as *a baby*. Bawa Muhaiyaddeen also speaks of it this way. Someone asked Bawa once what it felt like to be him. He answered by closing his eyes and making little kissing noises like a baby nursing. In this new life a baby is born in the heart. Purity comes and a playfulness, an ease, a peace. Gilani says this new heart-baby sometimes talks to the soul *in dreams*.[20] Bawa says that this baby knows the language of God. It understands every voice that floats on the wind because it is in unity and compassion.[21] This baby has none of the exclusivity of loving, the limits we learn and later, hopefully, unlearn from our families (the blood ties), our culture, religion, tribe, and nation. Bawa says humanity is "God's funny family." That's how the baby sees.

I saw this baby come into my father's eyes in the last weeks of his life in 1971. Everyone felt it. My mother died (she was sixty-four, lung cancer) on May 8, 1971. My dad died of a stroke on July 2, 1971, at seventy-two. In the time between (fifty-five days), Dad lost all judgmental tendencies. He met everyone with unconditional love. He would go out on any excuse to walk around and talk with strangers. He had unlimited time and attention and helpfulness for everyone. So beautiful. I see that opening in John Seawright's mother and father too. To hear Rev. Ryan Seawright pray outdoors in the wind at a June wedding, as I did recently, is about as much as a heart can stand. Bawa used to go out *rounding,* which meant riding in the passenger's seat of a car driving very slow and waving to people walking on the sidewalk. Sometimes I'd go along. When pedestrians would see his face, it was like they were struck full-power with one of those old searchlights from Second World War airfields. Then they'd recover and wave so tenderly, as to a baby.

The connecting extends to all living beings. My friend Stephan Schwartz tells of an old farmhand who could stand at the edge of a field and speak in a soft voice to a particular cow a couple of hundred yards away, "Number forty-seven." That cow, who needed attention from a vet, would detach from the herd and walk over. Pleasant (the man's name) would talk to the cow, looking in her face, about what needed to be done, how it would hurt but that it was for the best. The cow would then patiently endure what needed to be done, and he'd say, "That's good. Go on back now." Then he'd call another one, "Number twenty-four." Stephan swears that he was present many times when this happened.

Bawa went into the jungles of Sri Lanka for fifty years to watch the animals and learn about God. When your heart dissolves in this love, books are beside the point. We learn from the taste of life events. Jelaluddin Chelebi once asked me what religion I was. I threw up my hands in the *who knows* gesture. "Good," he said. "Love is the religion, and the universe is the book."

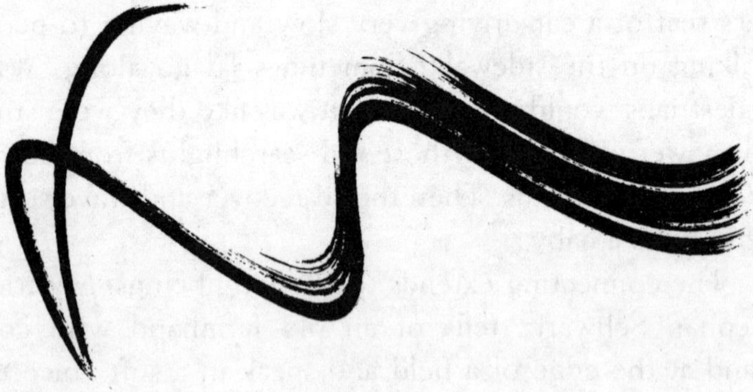

## ESCAPING TO THE FOREST

Some souls have gotten free of their bodies.
Do you see them? Open your eyes for those
who escape to meet with other escapees,

whose hearts associate in a way they have
of leaving their false selves
to live in a truer self.

I don't mind if my companions
wander away for a while.

They will come back like a smiling drunk.
The thirsty ones die of their thirst.

The nightingale sometimes flies from a garden
to sing in the forest.

Love comes sailing through and I scream.
Love sits beside me like a private supply of itself.
Love puts away the instruments
and takes off the silk robes. Our nakedness
together changes me completely.

## ANY CHANCE MEETING

In every gathering, in any chance meeting
on the street, there is a shine, an elegance

rising up. Today I recognized that that
jewel-like beauty is the presence, our loving

confusion, the glow in which watery clay gets
brighter than fire, the one we call the Friend.

## NASUH'S CHANGING

At that moment his spirit grows wings and lifts.
His ego falls like a battered wall.
He unites with God, alive,
but emptied of Nasuh.

His ship sinks and in its place move the ocean waves.
His body's disgrace, like a falcon's loosened
binding, slips from the falcon's foot.

His stones drink in water. His field shines like satin
with gold threads in it. Someone dead a hundred
years steps out strong and handsome.
A broken stick breaks into bud.[22]

If you love love,
look for yourself.

What I say makes me drunk.
Nightingale, iris, parrot, jasmine,

I speak those languages, along with
the idiom of my longing for Shamsi Tabriz.

## THE CIRCLE

Is there anything better than selling figs
to the fig seller?
                    That's how this is.
Making a profit is not why we're here,
nor pleasure, nor even joy.
                    When someone
is a goldsmith, wherever he goes, he asks
for the goldsmith.
                    The clouds build with
what we share.
                    Wheat stays wheat right
through the threshing.
                    How just do you
feel when you load a lame donkey?
The world has some share in this cup.
That's how it turns green.
                    Let the lean
and wounded be revived in your garden.

How would the soul feel in the beloved's
river?
Fish washed free and clean of fear.
You drive us away, but we return like pet
pigeons.
Ten nights becoming dawn flow
in us as a new kind of waking.
Shahabuddin
Osmond joins the circle! We will say
the poem again so he can play.
There is
no end to anything round.

# 7. Grief

The deeper the grief, the more radiant the love. We miss our friend. Lovers' tears are the true wealth. My friend John Seawright used to say that the real tragedy is when you don't feel much of anything when someone dies. That lack of grieving, *the feel of not to feel it,*[23] is not heard much in Rumi.

I recently saw *Fierce Grace,* about Ram Dass's life and particularly the stroke. The movie focuses on the use of the starkest tragedies, not just his, to open the heart and help us find the vital core of consciousness, the soul. My favorite part is Ram Dass near the end saying *yumyumyumyumyum* when he hears a young woman tell her dream of her lover who has been murdered in Colombia. Several months after her lover's death she has the first dream in which he has appeared. She yells at him, "Where have you been!" He says, *Listen. The love we had was wonderful, but that is small peanuts to what's ahead for you, and when that love comes, I'll be part of it.*

Ram Dass ecstatically tastes the *truth* of what the dead lover says. No sticky possessiveness, no hanging on to the past. Grief opens us to more love, and the new love builds with the former, and there's miraculous expansion. It's a rare movie that gives off the fragrance of enlightened love. This one does.

## THE DEATH OF SALADIN

You left ground and sky weeping,[24]
mind and soul full of grief.

No one can take your place in existence
or in absence. Both mourn,
the angels, the prophets, and this sadness
I feel has taken from me the taste of language,

so that I can't say the flavor
of my being apart. The roof
of the kingdom within has collapsed!

When I say the word *you,* I mean
a hundred universes.

Pouring grief of water, or secret dripping
in the heart, eyes in the head or eyes
of the soul, I saw yesterday
that all these flow out to find you
when you're not here.

That bright fire bird Saladin
went like an arrow, and now the bow
trembles and sobs.

If you know how to weep for human beings,
weep for Saladin.

## BIRDWINGS

Your grief for what you've lost lifts a mirror
up to where you're bravely working.

Expecting the worst, you look, and instead,
here's the joyful face you've been wanting to see.

Your hand opens and closes and opens and closes.
If it were always a fist or always stretched open,
you would be paralyzed.

Your deepest presence is in every small
contracting and expanding,

the two as beautifully balanced and coordinated
as birdwings.

## THE SILENT ARTICULATION OF A FACE

Love comes with a knife, not some
shy question, and not with fears
for its reputation! I say
these things disinterestedly. Accept them
in kind. Love is a madman,

working his wild schemes, tearing off his clothes,
running through the mountains, drinking poison,
and now quietly choosing annihilation.

A tiny spider tries to wrap an enormous wasp.
Think of the spiderweb woven across the cave
where Muhammad slept! There are love stories,
and there is obliteration into love.

You've been walking the ocean's edge,
holding up your robes to keep them dry.

You must dive naked under and deeper under,
a thousand times deeper! Love flows down.

The ground submits to the sky and suffers
what comes. Tell me, is the earth worse
for giving in like that?

Don't put blankets over the drum!
Open completely. Let your spirit-ear
listen to the green dome's passionate murmur.

Let the cords of your robe be untied.
Shiver in this new love beyond all
above and below. The sun rises, but which way
does night go? I have no more words.

Let soul speak with the silent
articulation of a face.

## THE ALLURE OF LOVE

Someone who does not run
toward the allure of love walks
a road where nothing lives.

But this dove here senses
the love-hawk floating above
and waits and will not be driven
or scared to safety.

## SKY-CIRCLES

The way of love is not
a subtle argument.

The door there
is devastation.

Birds make great sky-circles
of their freedom.

How do they learn that?
They fall, and falling,
they're given wings.

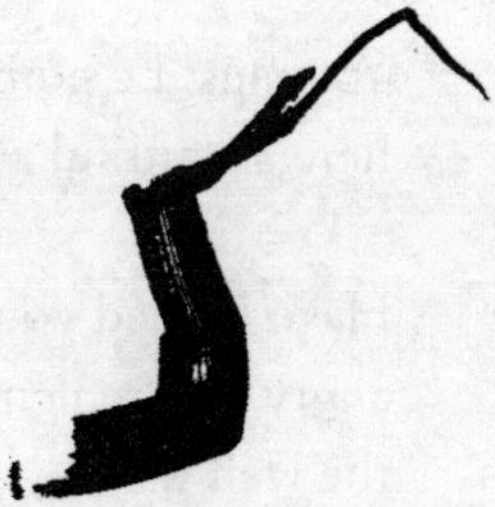

## I THROW IT ALL AWAY

You play with the great globe of union,
you that see everyone so clearly
and cannot be seen. Even universal

intelligence gets blurry when it thinks
you may leave. You came here alone,
but you create hundreds of new worlds.

Spring is a peacock flirting with
revelation. The rose gardens flame.
Ocean enters the boat. I throw
it all away, except this love for Shams.

## YOUR FACE

You may be planning departure, as a human soul
leaves the world taking almost all its sweetness
with it. You saddle your horse.

You must be going. Remember you have friends
here as faithful as grass and sky.

Have I failed you? Possibly you're
angry. But remember our nights of conversation,
the well work, yellow roses by ocean,

the longing, the archangel Gabriel
saying *So be it.* Shamsi Tabriz, your face,
is what every religion tries to remember.

I've broken through to longing now,
filled with a grief I have felt before,
but never like this.

The center leads to love.
Soul opens the creation core.

Hold on to your particular pain.
That too can take you to God.

My work is to carry this love
as comfort for those who long for you,
to go everywhere you've walked
and gaze at the pressed-down dirt.

Pale sunlight,
pale the wall.

Love moves away.
The light changes.

I need more grace
than I thought.

A certain Sufi tore his robe in grief,
and the tearing brought such relief he gave the robe
the name *faraji,* which means *ripped open,*

*or happiness,* or *one who brings the joy*
*of being opened.* It comes from the stem *faraj,*
which also refers to the genitals, male and female.

His teacher understood the purity of the action,
while others just saw the ragged appearance.

If you want peace and purity, tear away
the coverings! This is the purpose of emotion,
to let a streaming beauty flow through you.

Call it *spirit, elixir,* or *the original agreement*
between yourself and God. Opening into that
gives peace, a song of being empty, pure silence.

The ground's generosity takes in our compost
and grows beauty. Try to be more
like the ground.

Give back better, as rough clods return
an ear of corn, a tassel, a barley
awn, this sleek handful of oats.

# 8. *Tavern Madness*

There is an overwhelming contact with the divine called drunkenness. The tavern is a place of shared mystical *experience* as opposed to the church with its tradition of *received*, and sometimes unquestioned, belief (though churches can sometimes turn into taverns). The tavern is an excited region where one is out of one's mind, with others. The wine there is not an Australian merlot, but the shared sense of presence flowing through. The top of one's head blows. Majnun, the mad lover, sees Layla's dog and faints.

The tavern is no place one can live. Go to night prayers, then home. It is a state of stunned surrender that will eventually be left behind for the clarity of dawn. The tavern mystic must go "beyond the drunkenness of God's overwhelming and come to the clarity of sobriety, where contemplation is restored."[25] In the tavern one is absent and present at the same time. Junnaiyd says there is a sobriety that contains all drunkenness, but there is no drunkenness that contains all sobriety. In this region there's flailing about, sudden insight, physical danger, and miscommunication. Move, make a mistake. *Checkmate.* And the veils become fascinating here with their woven designs, the tapestries depicting long passionate stories about the hurt of separation, the consuming intensity of desire, love in the Western world.

Thich Nhat Hanh tells a wonderful story in his commentaries on the Buddha's Heart Sutra about how the opposites of good and evil only *seem* to oppose each other. He shows how they are actually great buddies who meet in the heart's tavern.

> One day Buddha was in his cave, and Ananda, Buddha's assistant, was standing near the entrance. Suddenly he saw Mara, the evil one, coming. Mara walked straight to Ananda and told him to announce his visit to Buddha.
>
> Ananda said, "Why have you come here? You were defeated by Buddha under the Bodhi tree. Go away! You are his enemy!"
>
> Mara began to laugh. "Did you say that your teacher has told you that he has enemies?" That made Ananda very embarrassed. He went in to announce Mara to Buddha.
>
> "Is it true? Is he really here?" Buddha went out in person to greet Mara. He bowed and took his hands in the warmest way. "How have you been? Is everything all right?"
>
> After they sat down to tea, Mara said, "Things are not going well at all. I am tired of being a Mara. You have to talk in riddles, and if you do anything, you have to be tricky and look evil. I'm tired of all that. But the worst part is my disciples. Now they are talking about social justice, peace, equality, liberation, nonduality, nonviolence, all that. It would be better if I hand them all over to you. I want to be something else."
>
> Buddha listened with compassion. "Do you think it's fun being a Buddha? My disciples put words in my mouth that I never said. They build garish temples. They package my teachings as items for commerce. Mara, you don't really want to be a Buddha!"[26]

Ananda continued to be puzzled and amazed by their conversation. The beautiful wholeness of it cannot be accepted by the mind.

I am a glass of wine with dark sediment.
I pour it all in the river.

Love says to me, "Good, but you don't see
*your own* beauty. I am the wind

that mixes in your fire, who stirs
and brightens, then makes you gutter out."

## SMOKE

Don't listen to anything I say.
I must enter the center of the fire.

Fire is my child, but I must
be consumed and become fire.

Why is there crackling and smoke?
Because the firewood and the flames
are still talking about each other.

"You are too dense. Go away!"

"You are too wavering.
I have solid form."

In the blackness those friends keep arguing.
Like a wanderer with no face.
Like the most powerful bird in existence
sitting on its perch, refusing to move.

## I'M NOT SAYING THIS RIGHT

You bind me, and I tear away in a rage
to open out into air, a round
brightness, a candlepoint,
all reason, all love.

This confusing joy, your doing,
this hangover, your tender thorn.

You turn to look, I turn.
I'm not saying this right.

I am a jailed crazy who ties up spirit-women.
I am Solomon.

What goes comes back. Come back.
We never left each other.

A disbeliever hides disbelief,
but I will say his secret.

More and more awake, getting up at night,
spinning and falling in love with Shams.

## WHO SAYS WORDS WITH MY MOUTH?

Who looks out with my eyes? What is
the soul? I cannot stop asking.

If I could taste one sip of an answer,
I could break out of this prison for drunks.

I didn't come here of my own accord,
and I can't leave that way.

Whoever brought me here will have to take me home.

This poetry. I never know what I'm going to say.
I don't plan it.
When I'm outside the saying of it,
I get very quiet and rarely speak at all.

We have a huge barrel of wine, but no cups.
That's fine with us. Every morning
we glow and in the evening we glow again.

They say there's no future for us. They're right.
Which is fine with us.

Real value comes with madness,
*matzoob*[27] below, scientist above.

Whoever finds love
beneath hurt and grief

disappears into emptiness
with a thousand new disguises.

## A CAP TO WEAR IN BOTH WORLDS

There is a passion in me that doesn't
long for anything from another human being.

I was given something else, a cap to wear
in both worlds. It fell off. No matter.

One morning I went to a place beyond dawn.
A source of sweetness that flows
and is never less. I have been shown
a beauty that would confuse both worlds,

but I won't cause that uproar. I am
nothing but a head set on the ground
as a gift for Shams.

Midnight, but your forehead
shines with dawn. You dance as

you come to me and curl by curl
undo the dark. Let jealousy end.

There's a strange frenzy in my head,
of birds flying,
each particle circulating on its own.
Is the one I love everywhere?

## FRINGE

You wreck my shop and my house and now my heart,
but how can I run from what gives me life?

I'm weary of personal worrying, in love
with the art of madness! Tear open my shame

and show the mystery. How much longer
do I have to fret with self-restraint and fear?

Friends, this is how it is: we are fringe
sewn inside the lining of a robe. Soon

we'll be loosened, the binding threads torn
out. The beloved is a lion. We're

the lame deer in his paws. Consider
what choices we have!

Drunks fear the police,
but the police are drunk too.

People in this town, we love them
both like different chess pieces.

## THE ACHE AND CONFUSION

Near the end you saw rose and thorn together,
evening and morning light commingling.

You have broken many shapes and stirred
their colors into the mud.

Now you sit in a garden not doing a thing,
smiling. You have felt the ache

and confusion of a hangover, yet
you take again the wine that's handed you.

Let the lover be disgraceful, crazy,
absentminded. Someone sober
will worry about things going badly.
Let the lover be.

## WONDER WITHOUT WILLPOWER

Love's way becomes a pen sometimes
writing g-sounds like *gold* or r-sounds

like *tomorrow* in different calligraphy
styles sliding by, darkening the paper.

Now it's held upside down, now beside
the head, now down and on to something

else, figuring. One sentence saves
an illustrious man from disaster, but

fame does not matter to the split tongue
of a pen. Hippocrates knows how the cure

must go. His pen does not. This one
I am calling *pen,* or sometimes *flag,*

has no mind. You, the pen, are most sanely
insane. You cannot be spoken of rationally.

Opposites are drawn into your presence but
not to be resolved. You are not whole

or ever complete. You are the wonder
without willpower going where you want.

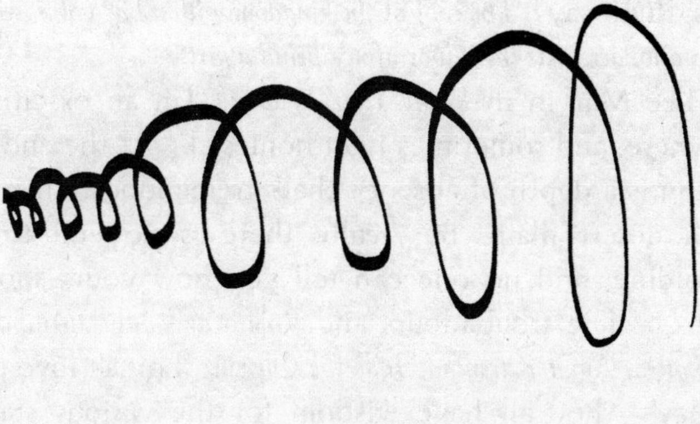

# 9. *Absence*

Love as a way into God is wild and bewildering. Union! Absence! What do these words mean? Attar says if you want to learn the secrets of love that your soul can know, "You will sacrifice everything. You will lose what you have considered valuable, but eventually you'll hear the voice you've most wanted to hear saying, *Yes. Come in.*"

Another Sufi, Junnaiyd, recommends that we JUMP! "Plunge headfirst into the ocean of your loving. Then look around patiently for the pearl that is yours."[28] This heart-region is a vast emptiness. Nevit Ergin calls it *absence.* Rumi explores the images of a desert night, an empty pot, a house with a broken door, the weaning of a child, the flute before breath comes through. When his friend Saladin dies, Rumi says, *The roof of the kingdom within has collapsed, and I can no longer taste the flavor of my being apart.*

Lee Marvin in *Paint Your Wagon:* "I'm an ex-citizen of nowhere, and sometimes I get homesick." At the end of our loving is a depth of absence that's tremendously familiar. A high desert plain. But really there is no end to love's unfolding, and no one can tell you how yours should or will go. The troubadours and *Romeo and Juliet, Anthony and Cleopatra, Anna Karenina, Jude the Obscure,* Lorca's love poems, Millay's, they all have wisdom for the various stages of love's progress. Rumi, Hafez, and Emily Dickinson have ideas and images for the annihilation of absence.

The Infinite a sudden Guest
Has been assumed to be
But how can that stupendous come
Which never went away?[29]

Some people entertain this guest in specific physical form for a certain amount of time. Be grateful for such a chance, but remember, everyone has in them the great love that Rumi's poetry comes out of. It is the given that never goes away.

You are an ocean in a drop of dew,
all the universes in a thin sack

of blood! What are these pleasures
then, these joys, these *worlds*,

that you keep reaching for, hoping
they will make you more *alive*?[30]

## LIKE LIGHT OVER THIS PLAIN

A moth flying into the flame says
with its wingfire, *Try this.*

The wick with its knotted neck broken
tells you the same. A candle as it diminishes
explains, *Gathering more and more is not the way. Burn,*
*become light and heat and help. Melt.*

The ocean sits in the sand letting its lap fill
with pearls and shells, then empty.
A bittersalt taste hums, *This.*

The phoenix gives up on good-and-bad, flies
to rest on Mount Qaf, no more burning and rising
from ash. It sends out one message.

The rose purifies its face, drops the soft petals,
shows its thorn, and points.

Wine abandons thousands of famous names,
the vintage years and delightful bouquets,
to run wild and anonymous through your brain.

The flute closes its eyes and gives its lips
to Hamza's emptiness.

Everything begs with the silent rocks for you
to be flung out like light over this plain,
the presence of Shams.

## CANDLELIGHT BECOMES MOTH

Inside a lover's heart there's another world,
and yet another.

Inside the Friend of this community
of lovers, an ear that interprets mystery,
a vein of silver in the ground, and another sky!

Intellect and compassion are ladders we climb,
and there are other ladders as we walk
the night hearing a voice that talks of forgiveness.

Inside Shams's universe candlelight itself
becomes a moth to die in his candle.

## THE BASKET OF FRESH BREAD

If you want to learn theory,
talk with theoreticians. That way is oral.

When you learn a craft, *practice* it.
That learning comes through the hands.

If you want dervishhood, spiritual poverty
and emptiness, you must be friends with a teacher.

Talking about it, reading books, and doing practices
don't help. Soul receives from soul that knowing.

The mystery of absence
may be living in your pilgrim heart,
and yet the knowing of it may not yet be yours.

Wait for the illuminated openness,
as though your chest were filling with light,
as when God said,
*Did we not expand you?* (Qur'an 57:4)

Don't look for it outside yourself.
You are the source of milk. Don't milk others!

There is a fountain inside you.
Don't walk around with an empty bucket.

You have a channel into the ocean,
yet you ask for water from a little pool.

Beg for the love expansion. Meditate only
on THAT. The Qur'an says,
*And he is with you.* (57:4)

There is a basket of fresh bread on your head,
yet you go door to door asking for crusts.

Knock on the inner door, no other.
Sloshing knee-deep in fresh riverwater,
yet you keep asking for other people's waterbags.

Water is everywhere around you, but you see
only barriers that keep you from water.

The horse is beneath the rider's thighs,
and still you ask, "Where's my horse?"
*Right there,*
*under you!*
Yes, this is a horse, but where's the horse?
*Can't you see?*
"Yes I can see, but whoever *saw*
such a horse?"

Mad with thirst, you can't drink from the stream
running close by your face. You are like a pearl
on the deep bottom wondering inside the shell,
*Where's the ocean?*
Those mental questionings
form the barrier.
Stay bewildered inside God,
and only that.

When you are with everyone but me,
you're with no one.
When you are with no one but me,
you're with everyone.
Instead of being so bound up *with* everyone,
*be* everyone.
When you become that many, you're nothing.
Empty.

## THIS TORTURE

Why should we tell you our love stories
when you spill them together like blood in the dirt?

Love is a pearl lost on the ocean floor,
or a fire we can't see,
but how does saying that
push us through the top of the head into
the light above the head?
Love is not
an iron pot, so this boiling energy
won't help.
Soul, heart, self.
Beyond and within those
is one saying,
*How long before*
*I'm free of this torture!*

# 10. *Animal Energies*

Any love: earth-love, spirit, the way of a man with a maid, the way of a dog with almost anybody, the way of a hawk with the wind, of a swan with a pond, of grandparents with grandchildren, of an ant with a grain of corn, of a lion with a gazelle, all the natural drawings-together lead eventually to annihilation. This is the mystery of the animal energies. Rumi says, astonishingly, "God lives between a human being and the object of his desire" (Discourse No. 44). This is radical theology to this day, when major crises have roots in sexual repression—the Catholic pedophile priesty boys; the Muslim enraged-at-women, dismayed-by-Western-ease-with-impurity vandals. We Americans have our own deadly-to-life versions of denying the horny animal energies. We lie a lot. We avoid the intimacy of truth. We make nice, blind to our own rage. When we start bombing, we overdo it and never consider the tremendous collateral damage as another form of terrorism. Very different, but still a terror.

I like to think of the first mystical poem as that figure incised, and painted, into the farthest wall of the cave called Les Trois Freres in southern France. The Animal. Joseph Campbell called him "god of the cave." He does the dance of human and animal at once, owl, lion, horse, stag, man. He incorporates them all visually and looks out at you with your own menagerie, who have gone *inward* far enough to meet his gaze. Animals can live inside the landscape without our noisy self-consciousness. When we turn and go with them as Whitman did, we enter a silence and a transcendence. We perceive through their eyes with their energies. This is a metaphor, a tremendously important one, as well as an experience.

Hazrat Inayat Khan says that seekers should "accomplish their desires that they may thus be able to rise above them to the eternal goal."[31] At the core of each person's nature are unique seeds of desiring, which flourish through the development of personality, not through any suppression of it. We are not to become pale renunciate ciphers with no wantings. The animals of desiring, the rooster of lust, the duck of urgency, the horse of passion, the peacock of wanting recognition, the crow of acquiring things, the lion of majesty, the zebra of absence (I made that one up), these are not to be thwarted but lived, transmuted, and incorporated. This is the art of forming a personality. Only when we live the animal powers do we learn that *those* satisfactions are not what we truly wanted. There's more, and we are here to follow the mysteries of longing beyond where they lead. The purpose of desire is to *perfect* the longings, for at the core of longing is the Friend, Christ, Krishna, the emptiness, wherever it was that Igjargajuk, the Eskimo shaman, was when he came back from forty nights on the ice floes with one sentence, "There is nothing to fear in the universe." The great love at the center of longing has no fear in it.

There is a witness who watches the obstreperous play of flame and eros and says, *This is the dance of existence.* A great mutual embrace is always happening between the eternal and what dies, between essence and accident. We are all writing the book of love. Everything goes in. All the particles of the world are in love and looking for lovers. Pieces of straw tremble in the presence of amber. Isn't that the deal? We're here to love each other, to deepen and unfold that capacity, to open the heart. And that means living in the witness, I'm beginning to see.

Hearing Rumi's poetry helps. He would say, though, that poetry can be dangerous, especially beautiful poetry, because it gives the illusion of having had the experience without actually going through it. He would periodically swear off the stuff. No more God poems, I want the presence. No more love poems, I want to *be* love.

This region of animal energies is where sexuality enters love's book most obviously, although eros, as Freud showed, is a powerful ingredient in many motions that draw us. Sex is as basic and nourishing to human beings as baking bread. Rumi implies as much in the heroic simile of the breadmaking poem. Lovemaking is going on everywhere among the forms, and in a startling variation of the golden rule he says, *Remember, the way you make love is the way God will be with you.*

Once in an informal moment (there were many) talking to a young couple about their love life, my teacher spoke to the young man, "You have seen the bull, how he goes and licks the cow before he mounts her. This is good. We can learn much from the animals." With me he counseled not cunnilingus so much as restraint. It always tickled him that my name was Barks. "The dog of desire," he would begin, "we can learn from that one, but we must not let him lead us all over town, pulling to sniff a piece of garbage, to a place where another dog has urinated, then to roll on a dead fish. He will drag us around like this if we let him; he will take over our lives. We must discipline this dog and sometimes tie him up in the backyard and give him only scraps." He had my number. *Do not neglect the licking,* though, is still my bullish theme.

Interesting in this regard are the names that Bawa Muhaiyaddeen had for three illusion-making capacities of human sexuality: *Suran,* the enjoyment of the images that come to one's mind at the moment of orgasm. *Singhan,* the arrogance experienced in that same moment, associated with *karma* and with the qualities of the lion. *Tarahan,* the pathway of attraction that leads to the sexual act; it is associated with the birth canal or vagina. The three powers are thought of as sons of Maya. It is fascinating that there are these ancient Tamil words for mental processes we have barely noticed in the West, the first two, at least.

Note. The reference above to "priesty boys" and "Muslim vandals" is very un-Bawa. Snide, divisive, pleased-with-its-clever-self remarks will probably not help bring us into one loving family.

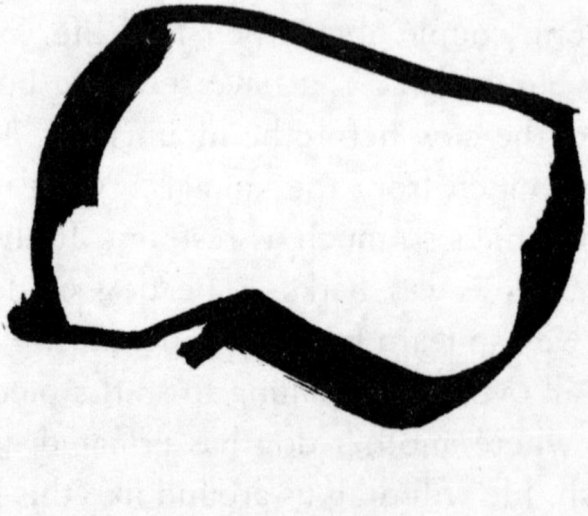

Think that you're gliding out from the face of a cliff
like an eagle. Think you're walking
like a tiger walks by himself in the forest.

You're most handsome when you're after food.

## THE PUBLIC BATH

Imagine the phenomenal world as a furnace
heating water for the public bath.

Some people carry baskets of dung
to keep the furnace going. Call them
materialists, energetic, fire-stoking citizens.

One of those brags how he's collected
and carried twenty dung baskets today,
while his friend has brought six!

They think the counting up at nightfall
is where truth lies. They love the smoke smell
of dried dung, and how it blazes up like gold!

If you give them musk or any fragrance
of soul intelligence, they find it unpleasant
and turn away. Others sit in the hot bathwater
and get clean. They use the world differently.

They love the feel of purity, and they have
dust marks on their foreheads from bowing down.

They are separated by a wall from those
who feed the fires, busy in the boiler room
belittling each other. Sometimes, though,
one of those leaves the furnace,
takes off the burnt smelling rags,
and sits in the cleansing water.

The mystery is how the obsessions
of furnace stokers keep the bathwater
of the others simmering perfectly.

They seem opposed, but they're necessary
to each other's work: the proud piling up
of fire worship, the humble disrobing
and emptying out of purification.

As the sun dries wet dung to make it
ready to heat water, so dazzling
sparks fly from the burning filth.

## *MASHALLAH*

There's someone swaying by your side,
lips that say *Mashallah, Mashallah.*

Wonderful. God inside attraction.
A spring no one knew of wells up
on the valley floor.

Lights inside a tent lovers move toward.
The refuse of Damascus gets turned over
in the sun. Be like that yourself.

Say *mercy, mercy* to the one who guides
your soul, who keeps time.

Move, make a mistake, look
up. *Checkmate.*

## SPIRIT AND BODY

Don't feed both sides of yourself equally.
The spirit and the body carry different loads
and require different attentions.
Too often
we put saddlebags on Jesus and let the donkey
run loose in the pasture.
Don't make the body do
what the spirit does best, and don't put a big load
on the spirit that the body could easily carry.

## BREADMAKING

There was a feast. The king was in his cups.
He saw a learned scholar walking by.

"Bring him in and give him some of this fine wine."

Servants rushed out and brought the man
to the king's table, but he was not receptive.

"I had rather drink poison! Take it away!"
He kept on with these loud refusals, disturbing
the atmosphere of the feast. This is how
it sometimes is at God's table.
Someone who has *heard*
about ecstatic love, but never tasted it,
disrupts the banquet.
He's all fire and no light,
all husk and no kernel. The king gave orders,
"Cupbearer, do what you must."
This is how
your invisible guide acts, the chess champion
across from you that always wins.
He cuffed
the scholar's head and said, "Taste!" and
"Again!"
The cup was drained, and the intellectual
started singing and telling ridiculous jokes.

He joined the garden, snapping his fingers
and swaying. Soon, of course, he had to pee.

He went out, and there near the latrine
was a beautiful woman, one of the king's harem.

His mouth hung open. He wanted her! Right then,
he wanted her! And she was not unwilling.

They fell to, on the ground. You've seen a baker
rolling dough. He kneads it gently at first,

then more roughly. He pounds it on the board.
It softly groans under his palms.
Now he spreads
it out and rolls it flat. Then he bunches it,
and rolls it all the way out again,
thin.
Now he adds water and mixes it well.
Now salt,
and a little more salt. Now he shapes it
delicately to its final shape and slides it
into the oven, which is already hot.
You remember breadmaking!
This is how your desire
tangles with a desired one.
And it's not just
a metaphor for a man and a woman making love.
Warriors in battle do this too.
A great mutual embrace
is always happening between the eternal
and what dies, between essence and accident.

The sport has different rules in every case,
but it's basically the same,
and remember, the way
you make love is the way God will be with you.

## SEXUAL URGENCY AND TRUE VIRILITY

Someone offhand to the Caliph of Egypt,
                    "The King of Mosul
has a concubine like no other. She looks like *this!*"
He draws her likeness on paper.
                    The Caliph drops his cup.
He immediately sends his captain to Mosul with an army.
The siege goes on for weeks, many casualties,
the walls and towers unsteady as wax.

The King of Mosul sends an envoy, "Why this killing?
If you want the city, I will leave and you can have it!
If you want more wealth, that's even easier!"

The Captain takes out the piece of paper. This.
The strong king is quick to reply,
                    "Lead her out. The idol belongs with
the idolater."
                    When the Captain sees her,
he falls in love like the Caliph.
Don't laugh at this.

Their loving is also part of infinite love, without which
the world does not evolve.
                    Objects move from inorganic
to vegetation, to selves endowed with spirit,
through the urgency of every love
that wants to consummate.

The Captain thinks the soil looks fertile,
so he sows his seed. Sleeping,
he makes love to a dream image of the girl,
and his semen spurts out.
He wakes up,
"I am in love."
His infatuation is a blackwater wave
carrying him away.
Something makes a phantom
appear in the darkness of a well,
and the phantom itself becomes strong enough
to throw *actual* lions
into the hole.
The Captain does not take the girl
straight to the Caliph. Instead, he camps
in a secluded meadow. Blazing,
he can't tell ground from sky! His reason is lost
in a drumming sound,
worthless radish and son of a
radish,
this cultivator tears off the woman's pants
and lies down between her legs,
his penis moving straight
to the mark.
Just then, there's a rising cry of soldiers
outside the tent.
A black lion from a nearby swamp
has gotten in among the horses.
The Captain leaps up with bare bottom
shining, scimitar in hand.

The lion is jumping twenty feet
in the air, tents billowing
like an ocean. The Captain splits the lion's head
with one blow.
Now he's running back to the woman.
When he stretches out the beauty
again, his penis
goes even more erect.
The engagement,
the coming together, is as with the lion.
His penis stays erect all
through and does not scatter semen feebly.
The beautiful one is amazed
at his virility. With great energy she joins
with his energy. Their two spirits
go out from them as one.
Whenever two are linked
in this way,
another comes from the unseen. It may be through birth,
if nothing prevents conception,
but a third does come when
two unite in love, or in hate.
The intense qualities
of such joining have consequences. Such
association bears progeny.
There are children to consider!
Children born of your sexual energy shared
with another are entities in the invisible world. They have
form and speech.
They are crying to you now.
*You have forgotten us. Come back!*
Be aware of this.

A man and woman together always have a spirit-result.
The Captain was not so aware.
He fell and stuck like a gnat
in a pot of buttermilk, totally absorbed in his love affair.

Then just as suddenly, he's uninterested.
"Don't say a word of this to the Caliph." He takes the girl
and presents her.
The Caliph is smitten.
She's a hundred times more beautiful
than he imagined! He also has the idea of entering her
beauty and comes to do his wanting.

Memory raises his penis, straining in thought toward
the pushing down and lifting up
that makes it grow large with delight.
As he lies down
with her, though, there comes a tiny sound
like a mouse might make,
a suggestion from God that he lay off these voluptuous
doings. The penis droops
and desire slips away.

The girl remembers the Captain running out to kill the lion with his member
standing straight up, then the running back.
Long and loud
her laughter. Anything she thinks of
only increases it like the laughing of those who eat hashish.
Everything is funny.
When she gets hold of herself,
the girl tells all,
the Captain's running about the camp hard as a rhino's horn,
then the Caliph's member shrinking
for one mouse-whisper.
The Caliph comes back
to his clarity,
"In the pride of my power I took this woman
from another, so of course someone came to knock
on *my* door.

The adulterer pimps for his own wife. When you cause
injury to someone, you draw the same injury
to yourself.
This lusting repetition must stop somewhere.
Here, in an act of mercy. I'll send you back
to the Captain.
May you both enjoy the pleasure."
This is the virility
of a prophet. The Caliph was sexually impotent,
but his manliness was powerful.

The kernel of true manhood is
the ability to abandon sensual indulgence.
The intensity
of the Captain's libido is less than a husk compared
to the Caliph's nobility in ending the cycle
of sowing lust and reaping secrecy and meanness.

## TWO WAYS OF RUNNING

A certain man had a jealous wife and a very
appealing maidservant.
The wife was careful not to leave
them alone, ever.
For six years they were never left
in a room together.
But then, one day at the public bath
the wife remembered she'd left
her silver basin at home.
"Please, go get the basin,"
she told her maid. The girl jumped to the task knowing she
would finally get to be alone with the master.

She ran joyfully. She flew. Desire took them both
so quickly they didn't latch the door.
With great speed
they joined. When bodies blend in copulation,
spirits also merge.
Meanwhile, the wife back
at the bathhouse is washing her hair.
"What have I done!
I've set cotton wool on fire! I've put the ram in
with the ewe!"

She washed the clay soap off and ran, fixing
her chador about her as she went.
The maid ran for love.
The wife ran out of jealousy and fear.

There is a great difference.
A mystic lover flies moment to moment. The fearful
ascetic drags along month to month.
The length of a *day*
for a lover may be fifty thousand years!
There's no way to understand this
with your mind. You must burst open!
Love is a quality
of God. Fear is an attribute of those who *think*
they serve God,
but actually they're preoccupied with penis
and vagina.
Rule-keepers run on foot along the surface.
Lovers move like lightning and wind.
No contest.
Theologians mumble, rumble-dumble, necessity and free
will, while lover and beloved
pull themselves into each other.
The worried wife
reaches the door and opens it.
The maid is
disheveled, flushed, unable to speak.
The husband begins his five-times
prayer. As though experimenting
with clothes, he holds up some flaps and edges. She sees
his testicles and penis so wet,
semen still dribbling out,
spurts of jism and vaginal juices

drenching the thighs
of the maid.
The wife slaps him
on the side of the head,
"Is this the way a man prays,
with his balls? Does your penis
long for union like this?
Is that why her legs are so covered
with this stuff?"
These are good questions.
People who repress desires
often turn, suddenly,
into hypocrites.

# 11. *Love's Secret*

Rumi makes preposterous claims. One of the most startling is, "Our loving is the way God's secret gets told!"[32] Love is an *open secret,* the most obvious thing in the world and the most hidden, with no *why* to how it keeps its mystery. Sufis say the genesis of lovers meeting is God's sweetest secret.

A saying of Muhammad is, *Human awareness is my secret and I am its secret. The inner knowledge of spirit-essence is the secret within the secret. I have placed this knowing within the heart of my true servant, and no one can know his state but I.* The knowing of essence is love's secret.

There is a truth that comes with following the energies, and there is a love, a truth-knowing essence, in the innermost heart. Rumi tries to lead us into this region that never fades and has no limits, that comes when we recognize that everyone is as precious as our own children and grandchildren. Bawa was clear with me that I needed to move beyond *blood ties.* Having children opened my heart, but he saw that I need to include *everyone* in my family. He so beautifully saw every human being he came in contact with as kin. *My love you, my children, grandchildren, brothers, sisters, mothers, fathers, uncles, aunts, great-grandchildren.* Every discourse began and ended with a declaration of the family connection.

Some may dismiss this as one-world, peacenik sentimentality. I'm not advocating we disband the armies yet, or even the churches, though that's tempting to say. It's good to have sanctuaries and singing and silence and Wednesday night prayer. We need more sacred space outdoors, though, fewer enclosed places, and please let's quit killing each other over books! Let's move on to killing each other over bluegrass and salad oil and circumcision and predestination and foreplay and whose uncle is the right line, where the prepositions go, and what happens after we die. Those are worth fighting for. The book thing is just getting *really* old.

Bawa Muhaiyaddeen says,

> Do not ever fight or argue, because for God there are no fights and no arguments. For that One everything is love; everything is in the form of love, compassion, and truth. May God provide you with the blessings and grace to live in that state.

## CLOSE TO BEING TRUE

How can we know the divine qualities
from within? If we know only
through metaphors, it's like when

children ask what sex
feels like and you answer, "Like candy,
so sweet." The suchness of sex

comes with being inside the pleasure.
Whatever you say about mysteries,
*I know* or *I don't know,* both are close

to being true. Neither is quite a lie.

## WHAT HURTS THE SOUL?

We tremble, thinking we're about to dissolve
into nonexistence, but nonexistence
fears even more that it might be given human form!

Loving God is the only pleasure. Other delights
turn bitter. What hurts the soul?

To live without tasting the water of its own essence.
People focus on death and this material earth.
They have doubts about soul water.

Those doubts can be reduced! Use night
to wake your clarity. Darkness and the living water
are lovers. Let them stay up together.

When merchants eat their big meals
and sleep their dead sleep,
we night-thieves go to work.

Love is the way messengers
from the mystery tell us things.

Love is the mother. We are her children.
She shines inside us, visible-invisible,

as we lose trust or feel it start to grow again.

## HIDDEN INSIDE

Hiding is the hidden purpose
of creation. Bury your seed

and wait. After you die, all
the thoughts you had will

throng around like children.
The heart is the secret inside

the secret. Call the secret
*language* and never be sure

what you conceal. It's unsure
people who get the blessing.

Climbing jasmine, opening rose,
nightingale song, these are

inside the chill November
wind. They are its secret.

How did you discover mine?
*Your laugh.* Only the soul

knows what love is. This
moment in time and space is

an eggshell with an embryo
crumpled inside, soaked in

spirit-yolk, under the wing
of grace, until it breaks free

of mind to become the song
of birds and their breathing.

If everyone could see what love is,
each would set up a tentpole in the ocean.

The world's population pitched and living
easily within the sea! What if inside

every lover's tear you saw the face
of the Friend: Muhammad, Jesus, Buddha,

the impossible-possible philosopher,
the glass diamond one, Shams Tabriz?

They try to say what you are, spiritual or sexual?
They wonder about Solomon and all his wives.

In the body of the world, they say, there is a soul
and you are that.

But we have ways within each other
that will never be said by anyone.

Come to the orchard in spring.
There is light and wine and sweethearts
in the pomegranate flowers.

If you do not come, these do not matter.
If you do come, these do not matter.

# 12. *Love's Discipline*

Rumi says an ecstatic human being is a polished mirror that cannot help reflecting. What we love, we are. As the heart comes cleaner, we see the kingdom *as it is*. We become reflected light. The polishing may be related to practices, a devotion we do every day that is an emptying out. Or it may be that when we live in the soul, everything can be used for clarity. Muhammad once said, "People who insult me are only polishing the mirror." I can't say precisely what *polishing the mirror of the heart* means, but I feel it happening slowly, and it does seem to be related to discipline, by which I mean intentionally giving time to what Rumi calls *the jeweled inner life*, which could be just the witness watching the mind.

In another passage Rumi says the polishing is done by the intensity of our longings. It is so difficult to remember who we are and to act from there. Various remembrance habits are helpful. *Zikr,* five-times prayer, a walk at sunset, twenty minutes of meditation. Stonework, singing, poetry. Find practices that are specifically *yours*. There comes then a creativeness at the end of the polishing that Rumi calls "looking into the creek." It's as though seeing becomes lucid dreaming. We watch the play of soul creatures. The gates of light swing open. We look in.

## WHO MAKES THESE CHANGES?

Who makes these changes?
I shoot an arrow right.
It lands left.

I ride after a deer and find myself
chased by a hog.

I plot to get what I want
and end up in prison.

I dig pits to trap others
and fall in.

I should be suspicious
of what I want.

## DROWNING

What can I say to someone so curled up
with wanting, so constricted
in his love? Break your pitcher

against a rock. We don't need any longer
to haul pieces of the ocean around.

We must drown, away from heroism,
and descriptions of heroism.

Like a pure spirit lying down, pulling
its body over it, like a bride her husband
for a cover to keep her warm.

## THE DOG PROBLEM

Now, what if a dog's owner
were not able to control it?

A poor dervish might appear: the dog storms out.
The dervish says, "I take refuge with God
when the dog of arrogance attacks,"

and the dog's owner has to say,
"So do I! I'm helpless
against this creature even in my own house!

Just as you can't come close,
I can't go out!"

This is how animal energy becomes monstrous
and ruins your life's freshness and beauty.

Think of taking *this* dog
out to hunt! You'd be the quarry.

## *ZIKR*

A naked man jumps in the river, hornets swarming
above him. The water is the *zikr,*
remembering, *There is no reality but God.*
*There is only God.*

The hornets are his sexual memories, this woman,
that, or if a woman, this man, that.
The head comes up. They sting.

Breathe water. Become river head to foot.
Hornets leave you alone then.

Even if you're far from the river,
they pay no attention.

No one looks for stars when the sun's out.
A person blended into God does not disappear.
He or she is just completely soaked
in God's qualities. Do you need a quote
from the Qur'an?

*All shall be brought into our presence.*

Join those travelers. The lamps we burn go out,
some quickly. Some last till daybreak.
Some are dim, some intense; all are fed
with fuel. If a light goes out in one house,
that doesn't affect the next house.

This is the story of the animal soul,
not the divine soul. The sun shines on every house.
When it goes down, all houses get dark.

Light is the image of your teacher. Your enemies
love the dark. A spider weaves a web
over a light, out of herself makes a veil.

Don't try to control a wild horse by grabbing its leg.
Take hold the neck. Use a bridle. Be sensible.
Then ride! There is a need for self-denial.

Don't be contemptuous of old obediences. They help.

## THE CORE OF MASCULINITY

The core of masculinity does not derive
from being male, nor friendliness
from those who console.

Your old grandmother says, "Maybe you shouldn't
go to school. You look a little pale."

Run when you hear that.
A father's stern slaps are better.

Your bodily soul wants comforting.
The severe father wants spiritual clarity.

He scolds but eventually
leads you into the open.

Pray for a tough instructor
to hear and act and stay within you.

We have been busy accumulating solace.
Make us afraid of how we were.

## CLEAR BEING

I honor those who try
to rid themselves of lying,
who empty the self
and have only clear being there.

# THE SOUL'S FRIEND

Listen to your essential self, the Friend.
When you feel longing, be patient,
and also prudent, moderate with eating and drinking.

Be like a mountain in the wind.
Do you notice how it moves? There are sweet
illusions that arrive to lure you away.

Make some excuse to them, "I have indigestion,"
or "I need to meet my cousin."

You fish, the baited hook may be fifty
or even sixty gold pieces, but is it really
worth your freedom in the ocean?

When traveling, stay close to your bag.
I am the bag that holds what you love.
You can be separated from me!

Live carefully in the joy of this friendship.
Don't think, *But those others love me so.*

Some invitations sound like the fowler's whistle
to the quail, friendly, but not quite
how you remember the call of your soul's Friend.

## LONGING

Longing is the core of mystery.
Longing itself brings the cure.
The only rule is, *Suffer the pain.*

Your desire must be disciplined,
and what you want to happen
in time, sacrificed.

The morning wind spreads its fresh smell.
We must get up to take that in,
that wind that lets us live.
Breathe, before it's gone.

## WHAT DRAWS YOU?

There are two types on the path, those
who come against their will, the blindly religious,
and those who obey out of love.

The former have ulterior motives.
They want the midwife near because she gives them milk.
The others love the beauty of the nurse.

The former memorize the prooftexts of conformity
and repeat them. The latter disappear
into whatever draws them to God.

Both are drawn from the source.
Any motion is from the mover.
Any love from the beloved.

## FEAR

Everyone can see how they have polished the mirror
of the self, which is done with the longings
we're given.
Not everyone wants to be king!
There are different roles and many choices
within each.
Troubles come. One person packs up
and leaves. Another stays and deepens in a love
for being human.
In battle, one runs fearing
for his life. Another, just as scared, turns
and fights more fiercely.

## A TEACHER'S PAY

God has said *Be moderate* with eating and drinking,
but never, *Be satisfied* when taking in light.

God offers a teacher the treasures of the world,
and the teacher responds, "To be in love with God

and expect to be paid for it!" A servant wants
to be rewarded for what he does. A lover wants

only to be in love's presence, that ocean
whose depth will never be known.

## LOOKING INTO THE CREEK

The way the soul is with the senses and the intellect
is like a creek.
When desire weeds grow thick,
intelligence can't flow,
and soul creatures stay hidden.
But sometimes the reasonable clarity
runs so strong
it sweeps the clogged stream open.
No longer weeping
and frustrated, your being grows as powerful
as your wantings were before,
more so. Laughing
and satisfied, the masterful flow lets
creatures of the soul appear.
You look down,
and it's lucid dreaming.
The gates made of light
swing open.
You see in.

## THE POLISHER

As everything changes overnight, I praise
the breaking of promises.
Whatever love wants,
it gets, not next year, *now!*

I swear by the one who never says *tomorrow,*
as the circle of the moon refuses to sell
installments of light. It gives all it has.

How do fables conclude, and who will explain them?
Every story is us. That's who we are,
from beginning to no-matter-how it ends.

Should I use the pronoun *we?* The Friend
walks by, and bricks in the wall feel
conscious. Infertile women give birth.
So beauty embodies itself.

Those who know the taste of a meal
are those who sit at the table and eat.

Lover and Friend are one being,
and separate beings too,

as the polisher melts
in the mirror's face.

# 13. *Shift from Romance to Friendship*

The story of the king, the handmaiden, and the doctor is of the movement from the erotic love of romance to the love of a meeting with the Friend, which is the mystery of this region. Rumi says that however we try to *explain* this new place, the explanation sounds embarrassing.

> Some commentary clarifies, but with love
> silence is clearer. A pen goes
>
> scribbling along, but when it tries to write
> *love,* it breaks! If you want to expound
>
> on love, take your intellect out
> and let it lie down in the mud.

As Shakespeare changed the verb *to be* forever, Rumi changed the noun *friend, dost* in Farsi. A meeting takes place that translates inner life into outer and outer to inner. The *sohbet* of Friendship is "the way messengers from the mystery talk to us." Call it Holy Spirit, Khidr, Buddha-mind, Friend, Beloved, or Lord, there's a shift from the romantic ache, which is a love dis-ease, to an encounter with "a person like the dawn," whose face loosens the knot of intellectual discourse. This Friendship breaks through the stalled-limbo of desire to become a reckoning (the astrolabe image) "that sights into the mysteries of God." Love changes from the exciting synapse of relationship to a condition of being, *the truest health.*

## BURNT KABOB

Last year, I admired the wines. This,
I'm wandering inside the red world.

Last year, I gazed at the fire,
This year I'm burnt kabob.

Thirst drove me down to the water
where I drank the moon's reflection.

Now I am a lion staring up, totally
lost in love with the thing itself.

Don't ask questions about
longing. Look in my face.

Soul drunk, body ruined, these two
sit helpless in a wrecked wagon.
Neither knows how to fix it.

And my heart, I'd say it was more
like a donkey sunk in a mudhole,
struggling and miring deeper.

But listen to me: for one moment,
quit being sad. Hear blessings
dropping their blossoms
around you. God.

## SITTING IN THE ORCHARD

A man sits in an orchard, fruit trees full
and the vines plump. He has his head
on his knee; his eyes are closed.

His friend says, "Why stay sunk in mystical
meditation when the world is like this?
Such visible grace."

He replies, "This outer is an elaboration
of the inner. I prefer the origin."

Natural beauty is a tree limb reflected
in the water of a creek, quivering there, not
there. The growing that moves in the soul

is more real than tree limbs and reflections.
We laugh and feel happy or sad over all this.

Try instead to get a scent
of the true orchard. Taste the vineyard
within the vineyard.

## THE PRINCE OF KABUL

Here is a story of a young prince who suddenly sees
that the ambitious world is a big game
of king of the mountain, a boy scrambling up

a pile of sand to call out, "I am king."
Then another throws him off to make his momentary
claim, then another and so on.

World complications can sometimes become
very simple very quickly, and age
has no bearing on this realization.

Neither are words necessary to see into
mystery. Just be and it is. A king
dreams his young son has died. He falls

into such grief in the dream that the world
darkens, and his body grows inert.
Suddenly he wakes into a joy he's never felt.

His son is alive! He thinks to himself,
*Such sorrow causes such joy.* It is a kind
of joke on human beings that we are pulled

between these two states as though with ropes
on the sides of a collar. Dream interpreters
say laughter in a dream foretells weeping

and regret; tears, some new delight. Now
the king has another thought, *What occurs
in dream can actually happen any second!*

If my son dies, I will need a keepsake.
When a candle goes out, you need another
lit candle. My son must give us offspring.

He's of marriageable age. I'll find
him a bride. This is flawless reasoning,
dear reader. Open any medical text and look

at the table of contents: tumors, rashes,
fevers, there are a thousand ways to die!
Every step takes you into a scorpion pit.

He found a wife for the prince, not from
royal blood or from wealth, but from a poor,
honest worker's family, with the greater riches

of an open heart. A beautiful young woman
clear as the morning sun. The women
in the court object vigorously, but the king

has decided. He knows the value of inner wealth
as opposed to the other: a long curving
file of moving camels, as against bits of hair

and dung. If you own the caravan, why bother
with refuse left behind? In a quirk of destiny,
as the marriage approaches, the old woman

of Kabul falls in love with the handsome,
generous-spirited prince. She enchants him
with Babylonian magic, so that he leaves

his bride at the wedding, and for a year
he kisses the sole of her Kabulian shoe.
Everyone weeps for him, while he laughs

in his ignorance. His father the king prays
constantly, *Lord! Lord,* and because of that
surrendered calling out, a master comes

from the road to save the prince. "Go to
the graveyard before dawn," says the master.
"Find the bleached-white tomb beside

the wall. Dig there in the direction
your prayer rug points. You'll discover
how God works." This story is long,

and you're tired. I'll get to the point.
The prince does as the master says and wakes.
He runs to his father carrying a sword

and a shroud, the signs his digging brought,
showing that he recognizes his mistake
and that he is ready for whatever

the consequences are. The king orders
that the entire city be decorated
to celebrate the new marriage. Such

an extravagant feast is prepared that sherbets
are set out for the street dogs! The prince
is so astonished by how the old woman

enthralled him, and by the return of his wisdom,
that he falls down in a swoon for three
days. Little by little with rosewater remedies

he wakes again. A year passes in this new life.
Then the king begins to joke with his son,
"Do you remember that old friend of yours,

how it was in her bed?" "Don't mention it!"
screams the son. "That was delusion.
I have found my real bride now." This prince

is the soul of humanity, your essence.
The old woman of Kabul is the color and perfume
of the sensory world. Release from the spell

comes when you say, *I take refuge with the lord*
*of daybreak.* The woman has great power.
She can tie knots in your chest that only

God's breathing loosens. Don't take her appeal
lightly. The prince was in her net for one
year. You might stay there sixty. You say

you grow restless when you don't drink the dark
world-drink, but if you could see a living one
for one moment, you would draw out that thorn

from your foot and walk with no limp. Let
the lamp of the Friend's face show you where
to go. Selflessness is your true self, sword

and shroud. Whereas this is how
most people live: sleeping on the bank
of a freshwater stream, lips dry with thirst.

In the dream you're running toward a mirage.
As you run, you're proud of being the one
who sees the oasis. You brag to your friends,

"I have the heart-vision. Follow me
to the water!" This love of spying far-off
satisfactions, this traveling, keeps you

from tasting the real water of where you are,
and who. Nearer than the big vein on your neck,
with waves lapping against you: *here, here.*

The way is who and where you already are,
sleeping in your very being: that which sleeps
and wakes and sleeps and dreams the sweet water

is the taste of God. Maybe another traveler
will come to help you see the stream,
like the man who laughs during a long drought

when everyone else is weeping. The crops
have dried up. The vineyard leaves are black.
People are gasping and dying like fish

thrown up on shore, but one man is always
smiling. A group comes to ask, "Have you no
compassion for this suffering?" He answers,

"To your eyes this is a drought. To me,
it's a form of God's joy. Everywhere
in this desert I see green corn growing

waist-high, a sea-wilderness of young ears
greener than leeks. I reach to touch them.
How could I not! You and your friends

are like Pharaoh drowning in the Red Sea
of your body's blood. Become friends
with Moses and see this other river water."

When you think your father is guilty
of an injustice, his face looks cruel.
Joseph, to the envious brothers, seems

dangerous. When you make peace
with your father, he will *look* peaceful.
The whole world is a form for truth.

When someone does not feel grateful to that,
the forms appear to be as he feels.
They mirror his anger, his greed, his fear.

Make peace with the universe.
Take joy in it. It will turn to gold.
Resurrection will be now. Every moment
a new beauty, and never any boredom.

Instead, the pouring noise of many springs
in your ears. The tree limbs will move

like people dancing who suddenly know
the mystical life. The leaves snap
their fingers like they're hearing music.

They are! A sliver of mirror shines out
from under a felt covering. Think how
it will be when the whole thing is open

to the air and sunlight! There are
mysteries I'm not telling you.

## THE WRIST

Who are you? The inner vision of consciousness?
The heart? A sacred half-light, are you that?

Do you grow gatherings? Are you a friend
of the sun, who comes and goes so quickly?

Do not forget your vertical passage,
the night of power,[33]
                                        and don't hide from the one
for whom all our secrets are down in the pillow under
his head, doctor of lovers, soul for
this thick world,
                                        the one who spirals iron
like dough and makes the body lightedness.

No belief is necessary to enter this tent
where one love story changes to another.

I remember that with these words brought here
by a falcon from the wrist of Shams.

If the beloved is everywhere,
the lover is a veil,

but when living itself
becomes the Friend,
lovers disappear.

## THE KING, THE HANDMAIDEN, AND THE DOCTOR

Do you know why your soul-mirror
does not reflect as clearly as it might?

Because rust has begun to cover it.
It needs to be cleaned.
Here's a story about the inner state
that's meant by *soul-mirror.*
In the old days there was a king
who was powerful in both kingdoms, the visible
as well as the spirit world.
One day as he was riding
on the hunt, he saw a girl and was greatly taken
with her beauty. As was the custom, he paid her family
handsomely and asked that she come to be a servant
at the palace. He was in love with her.
The feelings
trembled and flapped in his chest like a bird
newly put in a cage.
But as soon as she arrived, she fell ill.

He brought doctors together. "You have both our lives
in your hands. Her life is my life. Whoever heals her
will receive the finest treasure I have, the coral inlaid
with pearls, anything!"

So the doctors began, but no matter
what they did, the girl got worse.

The king saw
that his doctors were helpless. He ran barefooted
to the mosque. He knelt on the prayer rug and soaked
the point of it with his tears.

He dissolved to an annihilated
state. He cried out loud for help, and the ocean of grace
surged over him. He slept on the prayer rug
in the midst of his weeping.

In his dream an old man
appeared. "Good king, tomorrow a stranger will come.
He is the physician you can trust. Listen to him."

As dawn rose,
the king was sitting up in the belvedere on his roof.
He saw someone coming, a person like the dawn.

He ran
to meet this guest. Like two swimmers who love the water,
their souls knit together without being sewn, no seam.
The king said, "You are my beloved,

not the girl!" He opened
his arms and held the saintly doctor to him. He kissed
his hand and his forehead and asked how his journey
had been. He led him to the head table.

"At last,
I have found what patience can bring, this one
whose face answers any question, who simply by looking
can loosen the knot of intellectual discussion."

They talked and ate a spirit-meal. Then the king
took the doctor to where the girl lay.
The secret
of her pain was opened to him, but he didn't tell
the king. It was love, of course.
Love is the astrolabe
that sights into the mysteries of God. Earth-love,
spirit-love, any love looks into that yonder,
but whatever I try to say *explaining* love
is embarrassing!
A pen went scribbling along.
When it tried to write *love,* it broke.
If you want to
expound on love, take your intellect out and let it
lie down in the mud. It's no help.
Nothing is so strange
in this world as the sun. The sun of the soul
even more so. You want proof that it exists,
so you stay up all night *talking* about it.
Finally you sleep
as the sun comes up. Look at it!
Word of that sun,
Shams, came, and everything hid. Husam touches my arm.
He wants me to say more about Shams.
Not now, Husam.
I don't know how to make words make sense, or praise.
In the Friend-place nothing true can be said.
Let me just be here.
But Husam begs, "Feed me. Hurry!
Time is a sharp downstroke. A Sufi is supposed
to be a child of the moment! Don't say *tomorrow* or *later.*"
I reply,

"It's better that the way of the Friend
be concealed in a story. Let the mystery come through
what people say around the lovers, not from what
lovers say to each other."

"No! I want this as naked
and true as it can be. I don't wear a shirt
when I lie down with my beloved."

"Husam! If the Friend
came to you naked, your chest could not stand it.
Ask for what you want, but within some limits!"
This has no end.

Go back to the beginning,
the end of the story of the king and the lovesick
maiden and the holy doctor, who said,

"Leave me alone
with the girl." He quietly began, "Where are you from?
Who are your relatives? Who else are you close to
in that region?"

He held her hand to feel the pulse.
She told many stories mentioning many names.
He would say the names again to test the response
of her pulse.

Finally he asked, "When you visit
other towns, where are you most likely to go?"
She mentioned one town and another, where she bought
bread and where salt,

until he happened to say *Samarkand!*
The dear city sweet as candy. She blushed. Her breath
caught. Oh, she loves a goldsmith in Samarkand!
She misses him so.

"Where exactly does he live?"
"At the head of the bridge on Ghatafar Street."
"Now I can heal you."

The doctor went to the king
and told him only part of the story. "On some pretext
we must bring a certain goldsmith from Samarkand."

The king's messengers went and easily persuaded the man
to leave his town for a while. He arrived,
and the doctor said,
"Marry the girl to this man
and she will be completely cured." It was done,
and for six months those two loved and made love
and completely satisfied themselves with each other.
The girl was restored to perfect health.

Then the physician gave the goldsmith a potion,
so that he began to sicken. His handsomeness faded.
He became sunken-cheeked and jaundiced and ugly.

The girl stopped loving him. Any love based on
physical beauty is not the deepest love. Choose
to love what does not die. The generous one
is not hard to find.
But what about the doctor's
poisoning the poor goldsmith! It was not done
for his friend the king's sake.
The reason is a mystery,
like Khidr's cutting the boy's throat. When someone
is killed by a doctor like this one, it's a blessing,
even though it might not seem so.
Such a doctor
is part of a larger generosity. Don't judge his actions.
You are not living so completely within the truth as he is.

Reason has no way to say
its love. Only love opens
that secret.
                    If you want
to be more alive, love
is the truest health.

# 14. *Union*

The intensest, the most poignant cry comes from one who has known the union and lost it. Rumi says, *Give me his longing!*

I have seen one living in the state of union, at least one. They may exist in various guises all around us. Bawa Muhaiyaddeen[34] was totally present in each moment and so attentive to every detail, the tiniest bit of outer onion-skin left on a chopped bit, and also he felt with each breath the divine presence flowing through him. It was exhilarating to be there where he sat on his bed in Philadelphia, like breathing the ozone near a waterfall. He answered questions and listened to stories of what happened to people during their days. He laughed and tended business matters. He supervised the cooking of lunch, did the measuring and pouring in of spices.

Rumi says *lovers* are those who may seem to be judiciously considering very troubling matters, the world situation, relationship difficulties, "but really they're leaning back riding in a wagon on the Bukhara road, soul beauty their only expertise." That's the way it felt in Bawa's room. He was the most loving person I've ever met, and he had much to say about the innermost heart, the *qalb*. He lived there. He called it a house with ninety-nine windows (the qualities of God), a sanctuary, a flowering plenitude, a benevolence, a piece of flesh that does not die, the *kaaba* of the true pilgrimage, and source of the light that is the *ruh*, the soul. He also held that human beings cannot, and must not, judge one another's innermost heart. Only divine wisdom can do that.

The heart cannot be talked about. We must experience its depths in that mysterious osmosis of presence with presence. Hazrat Inayat Khan says that our purpose here is to make God a reality, a daunting and a potentially unbalancing task. One can get too full in the ecstatic state. Rumi warns that the roof is a dangerous place to drink wine. We can die *trying* to make God a reality. If we don't fall from the roof, we wake with a hangover that weakens consciousness. Hangover remorse can be helpful then. The work of balancing love (enthusiasm) and discipline (practical helpfulness) is beautifully addressed in the first poem of this section, the drink of water that is "The Sunrise Ruby."

## THE SUNRISE RUBY

In the early morning hour,
just before dawn, lover and beloved wake
to take a drink of water.

She asks, "Do you love me or yourself more?
Really, tell the absolute truth."

He says, "There's nothing left of me.
I'm like a ruby held up to the sunrise.
Is it still a stone, or a world
made of redness? It has no
resistance to sunlight."

The ruby and the sunrise are one.
Be courageous and discipline yourself.

Completely become hearing and ear,
and wear this sun-ruby as an earring.

Work. Keep digging your well.
Don't think about getting off from work.
Water is there somewhere.

Submit to a daily practice.
Your loyalty to that
is a ring on the door.

Keep knocking, and the joy inside
will eventually open a window
and look out to see who's there.

## THE GENERATIONS I PRAISE

Yesterday the beauty of early dawn
came over me, and I wondered who

my heart would reach toward. Then
this morning again and you. Who

am I? Wind and fire and watery
ground move me mightily because

they're pregnant with love, love
pregnant with God. These are the

early morning generations I praise.

## ONE SWAYING BEING

Love is not condescension, never
that, nor books, nor any marking

on paper, nor what people say of
each other. Love is a tree with

branches reaching into eternity
and roots set deep in eternity,

and no trunk! Have you seen it?
The mind cannot. Your desiring

cannot. The longing you feel for
this love comes from inside you.

When you become the Friend, your
longing will be as the man in

the ocean who holds to a piece of
wood. Eventually, wood, man, and

ocean become one swaying being,
Shams Tabriz, the secret of God.

Held like this, to draw in milk,
no will, tasting clouds of milk,
never so content.

## HANGOVER REMORSE

Muhammad said, "Three kinds of people
are particularly pathetic. The powerful man
out of power, the rich man with no money,
and the learned man laughed at."

Yet these are those who badly want change!
Some dogs sit satisfied in their kennels.
But one who last year drank ecstatic union,
the pre-eternity agreement, who this year
has a hangover from bad-desire wine,
the way he cries out for the majesty
he's lost,

give me *that* longing!

## SOUL, HEART, AND BODY ONE MORNING

There's a morning where presence comes over you,
and you sing like a rooster in your earth-colored shape.

Your heart hears and, no longer frantic, begins
to dance. At that moment soul
reaches total emptiness. Your heart becomes Mary,

miraculously pregnant, and body, like a two-day-old
Jesus says wisdom words. Now the heart
turns to light, and the body picks up the tempo.

Where Shamsi Tabriz walks, the footprints
are musical notes and holes you fall through into space.

Today, like every other day, we wake up empty
and frightened. Don't open the door to the study
and begin reading. Take down a musical instrument.

Let the beauty we love be what we do.
There are hundreds of ways to kneel and kiss the ground.

Out beyond ideas of wrongdoing and rightdoing
there is a field. I'll meet you there.

When the soul lies down in that grass,
the world is too full to talk about.

Ideas, language, even the phrase *each other*,
doesn't make any sense.

# 15. *Die Before You Die*

Death is key to this drastic change described in the last section. When we know in some deeply certain way that we are going to die, we move toward surrender more quickly. It is life's huge riddle, that we must die before we die, this dissolving into the heart. We shall certainly be changed in death, if not before.

Judge a moth by the beauty of its candle.

Shams is invisible because he is inside sight.
He is the intelligent essence
of what is everywhere at once, seeing.

### HUSAM

There is a way of passing away from the personal,
a dying that makes one plural.

A gnat lights in buttermilk to become nourishment
for many. Your soul is like that, Husam.[35]

Hundreds of thousands of impressions
from the invisible are wanting to come through you!

I get dizzy with the abundance. When life
is this dear, it means the source is pulling us.

Freshness comes from there. We're given the gift
of continuously dying and being resurrected.

The body's death now to me is like going to sleep.
No fear of drowning. I'm in another water.

Stones don't dissolve in rain. This is the end
of the Fifth Book of the *Masnavi.*

With constellations in the night sky, some look up
and point. Others can be guided by the arrangements:

the Sagittarian bow piercing enemies, the Water Jar
soaking fruit trees, the Bull plowing its truth,

the Lion tearing darkness open to red satin. Use
these words to change. Be kind and honest,

and harmful poisons will turn sweet inside you.

Lovers are alive to the extent
they can die. A great soul approaches

Shams. *What are you doing here?*
Answer: *What is there to do?*

## THAT QUICK

A lover looks at creekwater and wants to be
that quick to fall, to kneel, then all
the way down in full prostration.

A lover wants to die of his love
like a man with dropsy
who knows that water will kill him,
but he can't deny his thirst.

A lover loves death. Spill your jug
in the river! Your shame and fear
are like felt layers covering coldness.

Throw them off, and rush naked
into the joy of death.

## EMPTY BOAT

Some huge work goes on growing.
How could one person's words matter?

Where you walk heads pop from the ground.
What is one seed head compared to you?

On my death day I'll know the answer.
I have cleared this house, so that your work
can, when it comes, fill every room.

I slide like an empty boat
pulled over the water.

In the slaughterhouse of love they kill only
the best, none of the weak or deformed.
Don't run away from this dying.
Whoever's not killed for love is dead meat.

## I TRUST YOU

The soul is a newly skinned hide, bloody
and gross. Work on it with manual discipline,
and the bitter tanning acid of grief.

You'll become lovely and very strong.
If you can't do this work yourself, don't worry.
You don't have to make a decision, one way or another.

The Friend, who knows a lot more than you do,
will bring difficulties and grief and sickness,
as medicine, as happiness, as the moment

when you're beaten, when you hear *Checkmate*,
and can finally say with Hallaj's voice,
*I trust you to kill me.*

## IMADU'L-MULK

Remember the story of the king who is so enraged
with his close friend that he's about to kill him!

A privileged intercessor, Imadu'l-Mulk, steps in
and saves the man, but then the king's close friend,

who has just been saved, turns away and will not thank
the intercessor. A teacher comes and asks, "Why

do you act so strangely?" He answers, "I was in
the state Muhammad describes as *No other has been*

*this way with God, this near.* If the king wishes
to cut my head off, he may furnish me a new one,

or not. Pitchblack night in his presence is worth
a hundred festival days without him. Inside

the presence there's no religion, no grace, no
unfaithfulness, no punishment, and no language can say

anything about it, except that it is *hidden, hidden.*

You have said what you are.
I am what I am.
Your actions in my head,
my head here in my hands
with something circling inside.
I have no name
for what circles
so perfectly.

Some nights stay up till dawn,
as the moon sometimes does for the sun.
Be a full bucket pulled up the dark way
of a well, then lifted out into light.

# 16. *Harsh Evidence*

For Kharraqani and his wife love is conflict, *necessary opposition.* Two armies set the battle lines, a black flag here, a white flag there, then something happens between them. The Red Sea roars over both. Kharraqani's bossy wife is right for him. The heat of their being together gets a spring unfrozen and flowing again.

In this region love is a courtroom where harsh evidence *must* be brought in. Faithfulness must turn to betrayal and betrayal into trust before any human being can become part of the truth. Surely love is a big part of the truth we're here to live.

There's an ordeal, some anguish and suffering, essential to a soul's growing into deeper love. Life must be lived. One definition of Sufism is *joy at sudden disappointment.* The Sufis know that precisely the right disaster comes at the right moment to break us open to the helplessness that an opening of the heart requires. This is harsh truth, but the truth. Love grows near truthfulness, and fades when words are tinged with lying. Love grows from the ruins of personality. There are heart-regions that one does not enter willingly, or knowingly, and that one actively tries to avoid reentering. I don't use it much, and know very little about it, but the word *karma* may belong here, along with Auden's stanza,

O stand, stand at the window
As the tears scald and start;
You shall love your crooked neighbor
With your crooked heart.[36]

W. H. Auden is one of the best-loved poets in English for the very reason that he brings in the acerbic, the faithless, and the shadow within the deeply felt joy of his loving. There's an impending danger. To leave that dimension out of love poems is not to tell the full truth. Auden is gay, too, in all senses, which adds more depths to his cultural work.

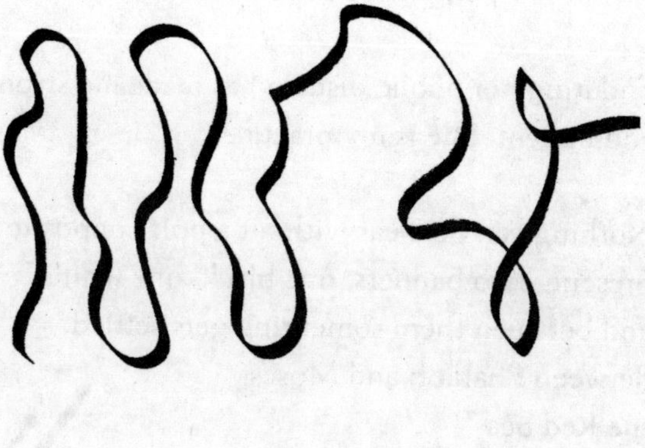

The young seeker wonders, *How could a teacher*
*lie with that woman!* Can a guide agree
with a thief?

Suddenly Sheikh Kharraqani[37] appears, riding a lion,
firewood stacked behind him. His whip,
a live serpent. Every master rides a fierce lion,
whether you see it or not. Know this
with your other eyes: There are thousands of lions

under your teacher's thighs and all of them
stacked with wood!

Kharraqani knew the problem and immediately
began to answer, "Well, it's not out of desire
that I put up with her! Don't think that.
It's not her perfume or bright-colored clothes.

Enduring her public disdain has made me strong
and patient. She is my practice.

Nothing can be clear without a polar opposite
present. Two banners, one black, one white,
and between them something gets settled.
Between Pharaoh and Moses,
the Red Sea."

## HARSH EVIDENCE

What sort of person says that he or she wants
to be polished and pure, then complains
about being handled roughly?

Love is a lawsuit where harsh evidence
must be brought in. To settle the case,
the judge must see evidence.

You've heard that every buried treasure
has a snake guarding it.
Kiss the snake to discover the treasure!

Don't run from those who scold,
and don't turn away from cleansing conflict,
or you will remain weak.

## THE STUPID THINGS I'VE DONE

Let your sunlight shine on this piece of dung,
and dry it out, so I can be used
for fuel to warm a bathhouse.

Look on the terrible things I've done,
and cause herbs and eglantine to grow out of them.

The sun does this with the ground.
Think what glories God can make
from the fertilizer of sinning!

## CANDLE AT NOON

A man is wandering the marketplace at noon
with a candle in his hand, totally ecstatic.

"Hey," calls a shopkeeper, "is this a joke?
Who are you looking for?"

"Someone breathing *Huuu,* the divine breath."
"Well, there are plenty to choose from."

"But I want one who can be in anger and desire
and still be a true human being in the same moment."

## DERVISHES

When school and mosque and minaret
get torn down, then dervishes can begin
their community. Not until faithfulness

turns to betrayal and betrayal into trust
can any human being become
part of the truth.

## DOVES

People want you to be happy.
Don't keep serving them your pain!

If you could untie your wings
and free your soul of jealousy,

you and everyone around you
would fly up like doves.

## WHEN WORDS ARE TINGED WITH LYING

Muhammad gave this indication of how to know
what's real. "When you feel

a peaceful joy, you're near the truth.
Unquiet and off center, jealous or greedy,

then what you do seems pretentious
and those around you insincere.

Speak the clearest truth you know,
and let the uneasiness heal."

When words are tinged with lying,
they're like water dripping into an oil lamp.
The wick won't light, and the pleasure
of your love room will diminish.

## THERE YOU ARE

You're inside every kindness. When a sick
person feels better, you're that,

and the onset of disease too. You're sudden,
terrible screaming. Some problems require

we go for help. When we knock on a stranger's
door, you sent us. Nobody answers. It's

you! When work feels necessary, you
are the way workers move in rhythm.

You are what is: the field, the players,
the ball, those watching. Someone claims to

have evidence that you do not exist.
You're the one who brings the evidence in,

and the evidence itself. You are inside
the soul's great fear, every natural

pleasure, every vicious cruelty. Someone
loves something, someone else hates

the same. There you are. Whatever anyone
wants or not: political power, injustice,

material possessions, those are your script,
the handwriting we study. Body, soul,

shadow. Whether reckless or careful,
you are what we do. It's absurd to ask

your pardon. You're inside repentance,
and sin! The wonder of various jewels,

agate, emerald. How we are during a day,
then at night, you are those moods and

the pure compassion we feel for each
other. Every encampment has a tent

where the leader is, and also the wide
truth of your imperial tent overall.

A night full of talking that hurts,
my worst held-back secrets: everything
has to do with loving and not loving.

This night will pass.
Then we have work to do.

There's a shredding that's really a healing,
that makes you *more* alive!

A lion holds you in his arms.
Fingers rake the fretbridge for music.

Dance, when you're broken open.
Dance, if you've torn the bandage off.
Dance in the middle of the fighting.
Dance in your blood.
Dance, when you're perfectly free.

All I know of spirit
is this love.

## YOUR DEFECTS

An empty mirror and your worst destructive habits,
when they are held up to each other,
that's when the real making begins.
That's what art and crafting are.

A tailor needs a torn garment to practice his expertise.
The trunks of trees must be cut and cut again
so they can be used for fine carpentry.

Your doctor must have a broken leg to doctor.
Your defects are the ways that glory gets manifested.

# 17. *Meditation Pavane*

This was my dream of August 10, 2001. I am a book in three parts. The first and last have generic, ineffable designations, *the beginning-less beginning* and *the endless end*. The middle part where (who) I am has an odd name that I see spelled out in capitals, MEDITATION PAVANE. Awake, I record the dream and think I have seen the word *pavane* before, though I don't know what it means, some kind of music? I look it up in the dictionary. "A grave and stately dance performed by couples in elaborate clothing, of Spanish and Italian origin, 15–16th century." A Mediterranean courtship dance, with a circle of elders observing. The word derives from a colloquial name for Padua and is related by folk etymology to the French *pavaner*, meaning to strut like a peacock. So a *meditation pavane* mixes the internal quiet of meditation with the social display of courtship.

There is a rare English word *pavonine*, meaning peacock-like or having the iridescence of their slender necks and the wide-open eyes on the tail feathers. Street pigeons sometimes have pavonine rings around their necks. I go to the Internet to search for *pavane*. The third item down has two familiar names, Barry and Shelley Phillips, friends of a friend, whom I will soon meet and do a bookstore Rumi reading with in Santa Cruz (October 2001). They are musicians specializing in Appalachian, Shaker, and Celtic melodies. Shelley has a CD called *Pavane.* Gourd Music is their label! I have published a volume of my own poetry, *Gourd Seed* (1993). I used to grow gourds.

The connections are clear. I call them to arrange some sound-studio time during my visit to Santa Cruz. That session turns into a CD, which we call *What Was Said to the Rose,* and also a concert in Santa Cruz (April 2002). The dance of courtship energies moving with the inner motions of meditation, let's say that mystery is the station of love explored in this section. The close-in irritation and excitement of the erotic, stepping with the cleansing of going-in.

The way we are led by dreams has been extremely important in my life. I have told the story elsewhere, several times, how I met my teacher in a dream on May 2, 1977. I'll tell it again: In my dream I am sleeping on the bluff above the Tennessee River five miles north of Chattanooga where I grew up. I wake up inside the dream, though still asleep. A ball of light rises off Williams Island and comes over me. It clarifies from the inside out and reveals a man sitting cross-legged with a white shawl over his head, which is bowed. He lifts his head and opens his eyes. "I love you," he says. "I love you too," I answer. The landscape, my first deep love, the curve of that river and the island, feels soaked with love, which is also just the ordinary dew forming in the night. I feel the *process* of the dew as a mixing of love with world-matter. That was the dream, and the only credential I have for working with Rumi's poetry. When I met the teacher in the dream, Bawa Muhaiyaddeen, a year and a half later in September of 1978, he told me to continue the work on Rumi. "It has to be done." Bawa died on December 8, 1986. I used to visit the Fellowship in Philadelphia several times a year for three or four days, over those nine years. He never asked for money in exchange for the wisdom he gave so generously. The curry was free too. Food truly does taste better when it's made by an enlightened being.

So let's have tea and look out at the cold sea. If you want one of these CDs that Barry and Shelley Phillips and I made (Irish, Appalachian, Shaker, and improvised music: cello, English horn, Irish harp, flute, with myself speaking Rumi poems, most of which are included in this volume), I'll send you one *free.* Call 800-682-8637. Leave your name and address.

## RULES ABOUT RESTRAINT

There is nourishment like bread
that feeds one part of your life

and nourishment like light for another.
There are many rules about restraint

with the former, but only one rule
for the latter, *Never be satisfied.*

Eat and drink the soul substance,
as a wick does with the oil it soaks

in. Give light to the company.

## THE COMPANY OF LOVERS

The rule that covers everything is:
*How you are with others, expect that back.*

If you want to know God, enjoy the company
of lovers. If you want to be thought a great

person, learn some subtle point and say it
with many variations as the answer

to every question. If you want to
live your soul, find a friend
like Shams and stay near.

## THE LOOK THAT OPENS

We wait for inspiration and ask no fee,
the feel of sacred ambiance being enough.

So bring your malaise, your dullness,
your callous ingratitude.

As we meet you, the coming together itself
will be medicine. We are the cure,
the look that opens your looking.

## STRAW AND GRASSES

*There is no reality but God,* says
the completely surrendered teacher,
who is an ocean for all beings.

The levels of creation are straws
in that ocean. The movement comes
from agitation in the water.
When the ocean wants the dry stems calm,
it sends them close to shore.

When it wants them back in the deep
surge, it does with them
as the wind does with grasses.
This never ends.

Friend, our closeness is this:
anywhere you put your foot, feel me
in the firmness under you.

How is it with this love,
I see your world and not you?

# 18. *Love Dogs*

The Sufis feel that dogs are our teachers with their faithfulness, their humility, and their bounding, unqualified welcome when we come home. The wordless intimacy of how we are with those beings teaches us to give ourselves wholeheartedly.

There's a *Saturday Night Live* sketch with John Lithgow as a Catholic priest hearing confession from actual dogs. A voice off-camera speaks for the dogs, "Father, I have barked at cats late at night. I have turned over a garbage can and eaten chicken bones." But Lithgow's face is so close to their faces and his intoning such, that the dogs begin to bark with the fun of it. It's hilarious, us forgiving them.

## THE OCEAN SURGE

I want to be in such passionate adoration
that my tent gets pitched against the sky!

Let the beloved come and sit
like a guard dog in front of the tent.

When the ocean surges, don't let me
just hear it. Let it splash inside my chest!

## LOVE DOGS

One night a man was crying *Allah! Allah!*
His lips grew sweet with praising,
until a cynic said, "So!
I have heard you calling out, but have you ever
gotten any response?"

The man had no answer to that.
He quit praying and fell into a confused sleep.

He dreamed he saw Khidr,[38] the guide of souls,
in a thick, green foliage.

"Why did you stop praising?" "Because
I've never heard anything back."

"This longing you express
is the return message."

The grief you cry out from
draws you toward union.

Your pure sadness
that wants help
is the secret cup.

Listen to the moan of a dog for its master.
That whining is the connection.

There are love dogs
no one knows the names of.

Give your life
to be one of them.

Inside water, a waterwheel turns.
A star circulates with the moon.

We live in this night ocean wondering,
*What are these lights?*

No better love than love with no object,
no more satisfying work than work with no purpose.

If you could give up tricks and cleverness,
that would be the cleverest trick!

## A GREAT WAGON

When I see your face, the stones start spinning!
You appear; all studying wanders.
I lose my place.

Water turns pearly.
Fire dies down and doesn't destroy.

In your presence I don't want what I thought
I wanted, those three little hanging lamps.

Inside your face the ancient manuscripts
seem like rusty mirrors.

You breathe; new shapes appear,
and the music of a desire as widespread
as spring begins to move
like a great wagon.

Drive slowly. Some of us
walking alongside are lame.

## BLASPHEMY AND THE CORE

My soul keeps whispering, "Quickly,
be a wandering dervish, a salamander

sitting in its homefire. Walk about
watching the burning turn to roses.

As this love-secret we are both
blasphemy and the core of Islam.

Don't wait! The open plain is better
than any closing door. Ravens love

ruins and cemetery trees. They
can't help but fly there. For us

this day is friends sitting together
with silence shining in our faces."

You're song,
a wished-for song.

Go through the ear to the center
where sky is, where wind,
where silent knowing.

Put seeds and cover them.
Blades will sprout
where you do your work.

Keep walking, though there's no place to get to.
Don't try to see through the distances.
That's not for human beings. Move within,
but don't move the way fear makes you move.

# 19. *One Stroke Down*

We sense an impending danger in ecstatic love, that the experience will change us radically. And it's true. The love-thief steals the keys to our favorite rooms, steals our half-loves. Ayaz crushes the pearl. There is a destructive downstroke when soul-love enters. The physical pearl and its value disintegrate to powder in the presence of the king. Tremendous courage and abandon come with Ayaz's act. The courtiers feel it and prostrate themselves, hoping for grace.

The progress in a story of Rumi's is toward a moment when consciousness breaks open and the Friendship is felt *here* and *now*. The ocean of wisdom becomes *this* weather we walk. Something like a jump occurs (though it may not be anything we *do*), and life is wildly different. You're naked and cold. Hallaj[39] says to dive in the river and get the fur coat that is floating by. You plunge in, and it's a live bear! There's the moment, a gamble one doesn't know or care how it will turn out. This bear is going to wear you home.

Lightning, your presence
from ground to sky.
No one knows what becomes of me,
when you take me so quickly.

I can break off from anyone,
except the presence within.

Anyone can bring gifts.
Give me someone who takes away.

The Friend comes into my body
looking for the center, unable
to find it, draws a blade,
strikes anywhere.

## WOODEN CAGES

I may be clapping my hands,
but I don't belong to a crowd of clappers.

Neither this nor that, I'm not part
of a group that loves flute music
or one that loves gambling or drinking wine.
Those who live in time, descended
from Adam, made of earth and water,
I'm not part of that.

Don't listen to what I say,
as though these words came from an inside
and went to an outside.

Your faces are very beautiful,
but they are wooden cages.

You had better run from me.
My words are fire.

I have nothing to do with being famous,
or making grand judgments, or feeling
full of shame. I borrow nothing.
I don't want anything from anybody.

I flow through human beings.
Love is my only companion.

## MORE RANGE

We're friends with one who kills us,
who gives us to the ocean waves.

We love this death. Only ignorance
says, *Put it off awhile, day after*

*tomorrow.* Don't avoid the knife.
This friend only seems fierce, bringing

your soul more range, perching your
falcon on a cliff of the wind. Jesus

on his cross, Hallaj on his. Those
absurd executions hold a secret.

Cautious cynics claim they *know* what
they're doing every moment and why.

Submit to love without thinking, as
the sun rose this morning recklessly

extinguishing our star-candle minds.

## AYAZ AND THE KING'S PEARL

One day the king assembled his courtiers,
He handed the minister a glowing pearl.
"What would you say this is worth?"
"More gold
than a hundred donkeys could carry."

"Break it!"
"Sir, how could I waste your resources like that?"

The king presented him with a robe of honor
and took back the pearl.
Then he put the pearl
in his chamberlain's hand. "What would it sell for?"
"Half a kingdom, God preserve it!"
"Break it!"
"My hand could not move to do such a thing."

The king presented him with a robe of honor
and an increase in his salary. So it went
with each of the sixty courtiers. One by one
they imitated the minister and the chamberlain
and received their reward of new wealth.

The pearl was given to Ayaz. "Can you say
how splendid this is?"
"It's more than I can say."
"Then break it, this second, into tiny pieces."

Ayaz had had a dream about this, and he had hidden
two stones in his sleeve. He crushed the pearl
to powder between them.
As Joseph at the bottom
of the well listened to the end of his story,
so such listeners understand success and failure
as one thing.
Don't worry about forms. If someone
wants your horse, let him have it. Horses are for
hurrying ahead of others.

The court assembly
screamed at the recklessness of Ayaz. "How could you do that?"

"What the king says is worth more than any pearl. I honor the king, not some colored stone."

The courtiers immediately fell on their knees and put their foreheads on the ground. Their sighs went up like smoke asking forgiveness. The king gestured to his executioner as though to say, "Take out this trash."

Ayaz sprang forward, "Your mercy makes them bow like this. Give them their lives! Raise their faces into yours. Let them wash in your cool washing place."

Ayaz in his speech
to the king gets to this point and then the pen breaks.

"You picked me to crush the pearl. Don't punish the others for my drunken obedience. Punish them when I'm sober because I'll never be sober again!

Whoever bows down like they are bowing will not rise up in his old self. Like a gnat in buttermilk, they have become your buttermilk. The mountains are trembling. The map and compass are the lines in your palm."

Husam, a hundred
thousand impressions from spirit are wanting to come through here.

I feel stunned in this abundance,
crushed and dead.

## HALLAJ

Hallaj said what he said and went to the origin
through the hole in the scaffold.

I cut a cap's worth of cloth from his robe,
and it swamped over me head to foot.

Years ago I broke a branch of roses
from the top of his wall. A thorn from that
is still in my palm, working deeper.

From Hallaj, I learned to hunt lions,
but I became something hungrier than a lion.

I was a frisky colt. He broke me
with a quiet hand on the side of my head.

A person comes to him naked. It's cold.
There's a fur coat floating in the river.

"Jump in and get it," he says.
You dive in. You reach for the coat.
It reaches for you.

It's a live bear that has fallen in upstream,
drifting with the current.

"How long does it take!" Hallaj yells from the bank.
"Don't wait," you answer. "This coat
has decided to wear me home!"

A little part of a story, a hint.
Do you need long sermons on Hallaj?

# 20. *Love's Excess*

Someone asked once, "What is love?"
"Be lost in me," I said. "You'll know love when that happens."
Love has no calculating in it. That's why it's said to be a quality of God and not of human beings. God loves you is the only possible sentence. The subject becomes the object so totally that it can't be turned around. Who will the you pronoun stand for if you say, "You love God"?

Prose Preface to Book II of the Masnavi

I, you, he, she, we,
in the garden of mystic lovers,

these are not true
distinctions.

SHAMS TABRIZ

The extravagant perspective of Rumi's life and work is that there is a core of understanding and that that core is love, the heart. Saint Augustine talks about "the supersensual eye of the soul." The eighteenth-century mystic Emanuel Swedenborg says there is a light that illuminates the mind that is different from sunlight, and that is what the word *enlightenment* refers to. Those who experience these other sights and other hearings are often in a state of untranslatable joy that almost dissolves them with its delight.

It would be strange if poetry written from such knowing were not excessive. Being *in the spirit* is not a casual thing. *Each ant is given its elegant belt at birth. This love we feel pours through us like giveaway song.*

It's not true, though, to say that Rumi's poetry always comes from a trance state. An enlightened being is most often very focused, present in the moment, and fiercely practical, even when saying the most mystical things. "You have to understand the form of the body in order to understand the meaning of the light form within it."[40]

And Rumi's knowing, like his father Bahauddin's,[41] has many valences, which certainly includes the *hulul*, or mystical trance.

## THE SOURCE OF JOY

No one knows what makes the soul wake up
so happy! Maybe a dawn breeze
has blown the veil from the face of God.

A thousand new moons appear. Roses
open laughing. Hearts become perfect
rubies like those from Badakshan.

The body turns entirely spirit.
Leaves become branches in this wind.

Why is it now so easy to surrender,
even for those already surrendered?

There's no answer to any of this.
No one knows the source of joy.

A poet breathes into a reed flute,
and the tip of every hair makes music.

Shams sails down clods of dirt
from the roof, and we take jobs
as doorkeepers for him.

## ROSES UNDERFOOT

The sound of salaams rising as waves
diminish down in prayer,
hoping for some trace of the one
whose trace does not appear.

If anyone asks you to say who you are,
say without hesitation, *soul*
*within soul within soul.*

There's a pearl diver who does not know
how to swim! No matter.
Pearls are handed him on the beach.

We lovers laugh to hear, "This should be
more that and that more this,"
coming from people sitting in a wagon
tilted in a ditch.

Going in search of the heart, I found
a huge rose, and roses under all our feet!

How to say this to someone who denies it?
The robe we wear is the sky's cloth.

Everything is soul and flowering.

## POETRY

I open and fill with love
and what is not love evaporates.

All the learning in books stays put
on the shelf. Poetry, the dear

words and images of song, comes down
over me like mountain water.

## BIRDSONG FROM INSIDE THE EGG

Sometimes a lover of God may faint
in the presence. Then the beloved bends
and whispers in his ear, "Beggar,
spread out your robe. I'll fill it with gold.

I've come to protect your consciousness.
Where has it gone? Come back!"

This fainting is because lovers want so *much*.
A chicken invites a camel into her henhouse,
and the whole structure is demolished.

A rabbit nestles down with its eyes closed
in the arms of a lion. There is an *excess* in
spiritual searching that is profound ignorance.

Let that ignorance be our teacher!
The Friend breathes into one who has no breath.

A deep silence revives the listening
of those two who meet on the riverbank.

Like the ground turning green in a spring wind,
like birdsong beginning inside the egg,
like this universe coming into existence,

the lover wakes and whirls in a dancing joy,
then kneels down in praise.

## EASTERN MYSTERY

I ask for the laughing, unconventional ones,
even them, to be broken,
for blood and sky to become one thing,
for revelation as startling as an ocean
that is neither wet nor dry.

I ask that lovers no longer be shy or concerned
with right and wrong, with reputation
or recognition. I have seen
the universal intelligence offer its neck
to the blade. I have asked why
and been told,
*Look around this gathering*
*and find those who resemble Shams,*
*who made Tabriz a source*
*of Eastern mystery like China.*

## NO FLAG

I used to want buyers for my words.
Now I wish someone would buy me away from words.

I've made a lot of charmingly profound images,
scenes with Abraham and his father Azar,
who was famous for icons.

I'm so tired of what I've been doing.
Then one image without form came,
and I quit.

Look for someone else to tend the shop.
I'm out of the image-making business.

Finally I know the freedom
of madness.

A random image arrives. I scream,
"Get out!" It disintegrates.

Only love.
Only the holder the flag fits into,
no flag.

# 21. *Love's Bewilderment*

Love loves flowing, a beyond-containment of blood and semen, wine and riverwater, amniotic fluid and the round bead of dew forming.

Flowering. Love cannot be held long within categories, likewise the poetry celebrating love. You might say that love loves confusion and not be far wrong. Love is metamorphosis, rapid and radical, agile, full of vigor and levity.

Love is the continuous alchemy of regions overlapping: animal, angelic, human, and the luminosity of the true human beings, their compassion and their cooking. None of this is sayable. It can only be lived. Rumi says, *Stay bewildered in God, and only that.* But the mind keeps questioning, turning away, *I don't think so.* There is strong resistance and fear and academic distancing in the rational precincts, which tend to mistrust any boundary-dissolving, beauty-relishing, ecstatic honesty.

God only knows, I don't,
what keeps me laughing.

The stem of a flower
moves when the air moves.

I reach for a piece of wood. It turns into a lute.
I do some meanness. It turns out helpful.
I say one must not travel during the holy month.
Then I start out, and wonderful things happen.

In complete control, pretending control,
with dignified authority, we are charlatans.
Or maybe just a goat's-hair brush in a painter's hand.
We have no idea what we are.

# MOSES AND THE SHEPHERD

Moses heard a shepherd on the road praying,
"God,
where are you? I want to help you, to fix your shoes
and comb your hair. I want to wash your clothes
and pick the lice off. I want to bring you milk
and kiss your little hands and feet when it's time
for you to go to bed. I want to sweep your room
and keep it neat. God, my sheep and goats are yours.
All I can say remembering you is *aaayyyyyy*
and *aaahhhhhhhhhhh*."
Moses could stand it no longer.
"Who are you talking to?"
"The one who made us and made
the earth and made the sky."
"Don't talk about shoes
and socks with God! And what's this with *your little
hands?* Such blasphemous familiarity sounds like
you're chatting with your uncles. Only something
that grows needs milk. Only someone with feet
needs shoes. Not God!"
The shepherd repented
and tore his clothes and wandered out into
the desert. A sudden revelation came then to Moses:

*You have separated me from one of my own.*
*Did you come as a prophet to unite or to sever?*
*I have given each being a separate and unique way*
*of seeing and knowing and saying that knowledge.*

*What seems wrong to you is right for him.*
*What is poison to one is honey to someone else.*
*Purity and impurity, sloth and diligence in worship,*
*these mean nothing to me. I am apart from all that.*

*Ways of worshiping are not to be ranked as better*
*or worse. Hindus do Hindu things. The Dravidian*
*Muslims in India do what they do. It's all praise,*
*and it's all right. I am not glorified in acts*

*of worship. It's the worshipers! I don't hear*
*the words they say. I look inside at the humility.*
*That broken-open lowliness is the reality. Forget*
*phraseology! I want* burning, *burning. Be friends*

*with your burning. Those who pay attention to ways*
*of behaving and speaking are one sort. Lovers who*
*burn are another. Don't impose a property tax*
*on a burned-out village. Don't scold the lover.*

The "wrong" way he talks is better than a hundred
"right" ways of others.
Inside the Kaaba
it doesn't matter which way you point
your prayer rug!
The ocean diver doesn't need snowshoes!
The love-religion has no code or doctrine.
Only God.
So the ruby has nothing engraved on it!
It doesn't need markings.

God began speaking
deeper mysteries to Moses, vision and words,
which cannot be recorded here. Moses left himself
and came back. He went to eternity and came
back here. Many times this happened.
It's foolish of me

to try and say this. If I did say it,
it would uproot human intelligence.

Moses ran after the shepherd, following the bewildered footprints,
in one place moving like a castle
across a chessboard. In another, sideways,
like a bishop.
Now surging like a wave cresting,
now sliding down like a fish,
with always his feet
making geomancy symbols in the sand,
recording his
wandering state.
Moses finally caught up with him.
"I was wrong. God has revealed to me that there are
no rules for worship. Say whatever and however
your loving tells you to.
Your sweetest blasphemy
is the truest devotion. Through you a whole world
is freed.
Loosen your tongue and don't worry
what comes out. It's all the light of the spirit."

The shepherd replied, "Moses, Moses,
I've gone beyond even that.
You applied the whip,
and my horse shied and jumped out of itself.
The divine nature and my human nature came together.
Bless your scolding hand.
I can't say what has happened.
What I'm saying now is not my real condition.
It can't be said."
The shepherd grew quiet.
When you look in a mirror, you see yourself,
not the state of the mirror.
The flute player
gives breath into a flute, and who makes the music?
The flute player!
Whenever you speak praise
or thanksgiving to God, it's always like
this dear shepherd's simplicity.

The minute I heard my first love story
I started looking for you, not knowing
how blind that was.

Lovers don't finally meet somewhere.
They're in each other all along.

## MORNING WIND

Wine so bitter all bitterness sweetens,
a beautiful face growing old.
The taste of
Khidr's spring, words that plant olive trees.
A man like the dawn
with a small suggestion,
*You should visit a few times.*
A prayer
at the graveside that resurrects the dead,
silence telling half a secret, unspoken wish.
Morning wind,
we'll stay quiet. Whatever
you have understood of us, go and tell that
to the living,
what we've been hiding from them.

## THE OCEAN'S MOTION

Love is an ocean. This wide sky,
a bit of foam on that.
Restless as Zuleikha
in her desire for Joseph,
sky-changes move across
day and night. If there were no love,
everything would freeze and be
still. Instead,
inorganic grains are entering
plants. Plants enter animals;

animals enter
spirit, and spirit sacrifices itself
for one breath
of that which made Mary with child. Each
sapling lifts, and the universe
winds like a locust swarm its wingrush
toward perfection,
each particle purified
in a song of praise for motion.

## IGNORANCE

I didn't know love would make me this
crazy, with my eyes
like the river Ceyhun
carrying me in its rapids
out to sea,
where every bit
of shattered boat
sinks to the bottom.

An alligator lifts its head and swallows
the ocean, then the ocean
floor becomes
a desert covering
the alligator in
sand drifts.
Changes *do*
happen. I do not know *how,*
or *what remains* of what

has disappeared
into the absolute.
I hear so many stories
and explanations, but I keep quiet,
because I don't know anything,
and because something I swallowed
in the ocean
has made me completely content
with ignorance.

# 22. *Lord of the Heart*

Love is our aloneness with the lord of such beauty and depth that we're not lonely. The empty space of the guest house, not the guests moving through, the host and theater where mind and desire play out their myriad motions. As say *Shakespeare* is the great globe itself, not the players, nor the drowned book, not the jealous lover or the eloquently introspective athlete or the rugged king, who calls himself "old and foolish," rather the space those inhabit and the source. This love-region called *lord* is not imagination. This emptiness so dazzlingly full of emanation is what gnostics call the *pleroma.* Niffari calls it *Ignorance.* Someone else, *the cloud of unknowing.*

Words do not approach it hence the edge of self-satire that word-mystics barely keep in check. This is the one we know early on in life and come back to late. Riverlord, director of dreams, the company that most nourishes our soul, this is the great love we're given and feel bearing us along.

It's not fair to speak as though this were everyone's experience, because it isn't, and I do honor the pained vision, the bitter childhoods, the broken trust. Rumi focuses not so much on the nobility of suffering or its heartbreaking howl as on the ultimate expansion into mystery that this poetry tries to say. It began with the Friendship with Shams Tabriz. It is still unfolding, and as many of the poems imply, the unfolding is intimately woven in with seeing. John Ruskin says,

The greatest thing a human soul ever does in this world is to see something and tell what he saw in a plain way. To see clearly is poetry, prophecy, and religion all in one.[42]

Bawa says something very similar.

Everything you see tells the story of God. Look at it. God is out spread, filling the entire universe. So look. You exist in a form. God is without form. You are the visible example, the sun. God is the light within the sun.[43]

I am so small I can barely be seen.
How can this great love be inside me?

*Look at your eyes. They are small,*
*but they see enormous things.*

## EYES

What is it that *sees* when vision is clear?
The core that has no story, has that ever *seen* anything?

Surely vision has loyalties.
Someone buying eye medicine does not see well,
but well enough, at least, to choose the cure.

Beyond day and night one watches
as your eyes close and open and close, as night
turning day turns night, as eyes
like particles float
in the light that is your face,
that is the sun.

Without you our eyes might be a danger
to the soul, but *with* you they become the same
as the soul. When that happens,
the heart is seeing!

You can *say* that the eyes see God, but it is God
who sees, as in the Qur'an when the desert mountain
looks at God, and eyes appear on every stone.

I am filled with you.
Skin, blood, bone, brain, and soul.
There's no room for lack of trust, or trust.
Nothing in this existence but that existence.

When you feel your lips becoming infinite
and sweet, like a moon in a sky,
when you feel that spaciousness inside,
Shams of Tabriz will be there too.

## THE GRANARY

Sufi masters are those whose spirits existed
before the world. Before the body,
they lived many lifetimes. Before seeds
went into the ground, they harvested wheat.

Before there was an ocean, they strung pearls.
While the great meeting was going on
about bringing human beings into existence,
they stood up to their chins in wisdom-water.

When some of the angels opposed creation,
the Sufi masters laughed and clapped
among themselves. Before materiality,
they knew what it was like to be trapped

inside matter. Before there was a night sky,
they saw Saturn. Before wheat grains,
they tasted bread. With no mind, they thought.
Immediate intuition to them is the simplest act,
what to others would be epiphany. Much
of our thought is of the past or the future.
They're free of those. Before a mine is dug,
they judge coins. Before vineyards, they know

the excitements to come. In July they feel
December. In unbroken sunlight, they find
shade. In *fana,* the state where objects
dissolve, they recognize things and comment

rationally. The open sky drinks from their
circling cup. The sun wears the gold of their
generosity. When two of them meet, they
are no longer two. They are one and six

hundred thousand. The ocean waves are their
closest likeness, when wind makes from unity
the numerous. This happened to the sun and it
broke into rays through the window, into bodies.

The disc of the sun does exist, but if you see
only the ray-bodies, you may have doubts.
The human-divine combinations are a oneness.
Plurality, the apparent separation into rays.

Friend, we're traveling together. Throw off
your tiredness. Let me show you one tiny spot
of the beauty that can't be spoken. I'm like
an ant that's gotten into the granary,
ludicrously happy, and trying to lug out
a grain that's way too big.

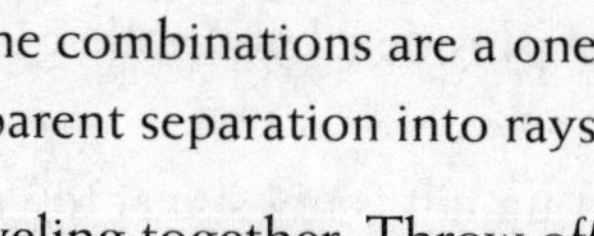

## THE GAZING-HOUSE

On the night when you cross the street
from your shop and your house to the cemetery,

you'll hear me hailing you from inside
the open grave, and you'll realize
how we've always been together.

I am the clear consciousness core
of your being, the same in ecstasy
as in self-hating fatigue.

That night, when you escape the fear of snakebite
and all irritation with the ants, you'll hear
my familiar voice, see the candle being lit,
smell the incense and the surprise meal fixed
by the lover inside all your other lovers.

This heart tumult is my signal to you igniting
in the tomb, so don't fuss with the shroud
and the graveyard road dust. Those get ripped
open and washed away in the music of our meeting.

And don't look for me in a human shape!
I am inside your looking. No room for form
with love this strong.
                    Beat the drum and let
the poets speak. This is a day of purification
for those who are already mature and initiated
into what love is.

No need to wait until we die!
There's more to want here than money and being
famous and bites of roasted meat.
Now, what
shall we call this new kind of gazing-house
that has opened in our town where people
sit quietly and pour out their glancing
like light, like answering?

## THE GUEST HOUSE

This being human is a guest house.
Every morning a new arrival.

A joy, a depression, a meanness,
some momentary awareness comes
as an unexpected visitor.

Welcome and entertain them all!
Even if they're a crowd of sorrows,
who violently sweep your house
empty of its furniture, still,
treat each guest honorably.
He may be clearing you out
for some new delight.

The dark thought, the shame, the malice,
meet them at the door laughing
and invite them in.

Be grateful for whoever comes,
because each has been sent
as a guide from beyond.

Always check your inner state
with the lord of your heart.

Copper doesn't know it's copper,
until it's changing to gold.

Your loving doesn't know majesty,
until it knows its helplessness.

# THE ONE THING YOU MUST DO

There is one thing in this world you must never forget to do. If you forget everything else and not this, there's nothing to worry about, but if you remember everything else and forget this, then you will have done nothing in your life.

It's as if a king has sent you to some country to do a task, and you perform a hundred other services, but not the one he sent you to do. So human beings come to this world to do *particular* work. That work is the purpose, and each is specific to the person. If you don't do it, it's as though a priceless Indian sword were used to slice rotten meat. It's a golden bowl being used to cook turnips, when one filing from the bowl could buy a hundred suitable pots. It's like a knife of the finest tempering nailed into a wall to hang things on.

You say, "But look, I'm using it. It's not lying idle." Do you hear how ridiculous that sounds? For a penny an iron nail could be bought. You say, "But I spend my energies on lofty projects. I study philosophy and jurisprudence, logic, astronomy, and medicine." But consider why you do those things. They are all branches of yourself and your impressiveness.

Remember the deep root of your being, the presence of your lord. Give yourself to the one who already owns your breath and your moments. If you don't, you'll be like the man who takes a ceremonial dagger and hammers it into a post for a peg to hold his dipper gourd. You'll be wasting valuable keenness and forgetting your dignity and purpose.

## THIS WE HAVE NOW

This we have now
is not imagination.

This is not grief,
or joy, not a judging state,
or an elation, or a sadness.

Those come and go.
This is the presence
that doesn't.

It's dawn, Husam,
here in the splendor of coral,
inside the Friend, in the simple truth
of what Hallaj said.

What else could human beings want?

When grapes turn to wine,
they're wanting this.

When the night sky pours by,
it's really a crowd of beggars,
and they all want some of this.

This we are now
created the body, cell by cell,
like bees building a honeycomb.

The human body and the universe
grew from this, not this
from the universe and the human body.

# *A Note on Translation*

I wonder, wonder, whom de doo doo—who
BOOM,
who wrote the book of love.

The Monotones out of New Jersey asked that musical question in 1957, and my name may be on the cover of this one, but I am not the one they're looking for. Jelaluddin Rumi wrote the book of love. What he loves is the source of any truth and beauty coming through here. The distortions are mine.

You can never be sure, though, what is, and is not, transmitted in collaborative translation, or any translation, version, imitation, whatever you choose to call the bringing-over from one language and time into another. It's always a failure of one magnitude or another. Think of translating *Hamlet* into Chinese, or Faulkner into Farsi, Poe into Polish. It can't be done, but the attempt must be made. The same with Rumi into American.

I'll try to describe what I do. I look at one text in English and write another. For example, I did a collection of poems by a fourteenth-century Kashmiri woman named Lalla, or Lalleshwari. The Naked Song poems came down in oral tradition for four hundred years before they were written down at all, some in Sanskrit, some in Kashmiri, some in both. Hundreds of lines from her poems are still actively a part of Kashmiri conversation. I don't read Kashmiri or Sanskrit, but Sir George Grierson and Lionel Barnett of the Royal Asiatic Society did read those languages. They published a book in 1920, *Lalla-Vakyana, The Wise Sayings of Lal Ded, A Mystic Poetess of Ancient Kashmir.* I looked at their book and the others listed in the back of mine to produce the text. I hope the words in it are some kin to Lalla's daring, darling, wandering songs. It's a process of attunement for me. There are many mystics that I cannot make versions of, because I don't feel connected enough to their words. Lionel and Sir George were not trying for that kind of closeness. On the contrary, they cultivated scholarly distance. Detachment was valued, and I am very grateful for their diligence and for the lifelong British stamina and scholarly passion of Reynold Nicholson and A. J. Arberry, the Cambridge Islamicists who brought Rumi to the West with their translations from the 1920s through the 1950s. My friend John Moyne has also sent me texts to work with over the years, and Nevit Ergin is another treasure. He has worked since the late 1950s to bring the entire *Shams* (Rumi's large collection of *ghazal*s and quatrains, the *Divani Shamsi Tabriz*) out of Golpinarli's Turkish into English. (Nevit Ergin's translations are available from Words Distribution, 7900 Edgewater Drive, Oakland, CA 94621. Also from maypopbooks.com and 800–682–8637.) Now the work of bringing the complete text from Farsi to English must be done.

With Rumi I try to enter the ecstatic consciousness, the love that is the subject that generates the poetry. I move with the images and try to absorb the soul-growth truth being transmitted. When it feels like a connection has occurred, the words come quickly, and at the end I feel my head bowing in gratitude. It has been an almost daily practice for twenty-seven years.

Rumi's poetry was a continuous spontaneous outpouring. The poems have no titles in Persian. They are seamless, whereas I have given most of these titles. In English we feel the title is an organic part of the poem, but it may contribute here to a false feeling of a stop-start process. There are no full stops. Rumi's poetry should be felt as a whole like Whitman's *Leaves of Grass* or Wallace Stevens's *Harmonium*. Also, in this collection I often take what I hear as the tastiest lines from a poem without giving the context. That can be found in the earlier volumes, *The Essential Rumi* and *The Soul of Rumi*. The wider truth is that Rumi's poems all grow together in a field called the *qalb*, or the innermost heart.

This volume is an attempt to present poems in a handier, more visually spacious form than I did in the previous volumes. It is a book designed specifically for those whom Rumi calls lovers, who are often on the move and need a travel size. There are new poems here, fifteen of them, but this is mostly a recollecting, a revising and relineating in some instances, of poems published in the other Harper San Francisco volumes.

# Notes

PREFACE

1. Oceanfrog: Bawa Muhaiyaddeen told this version of a Sufi story. An oceanfrog comes to visit a ditchfrog, who is very proud of where he lives, a section of ditch two feet deep, four feet long, and three feet across. He jumps around demonstrating the elegant spaciousness of his place. "How do you like this?" "Very fine," says the oceanfrog. "What's it like where you live?" asks the ditchfrog; he has never seen or heard of the ocean. "I can't really describe how it is where I live. Someday I'll take you there." I had asked Bawa what the difference was between my consciousness and his. "Someone who lives in the confines of mind and desire is like the ditchfrog. The oceanfrog swims the ocean of grace. It is good for them to visit each other."

INTRODUCTION

2. The heart as "the comprehensive human reality": quoted from Hasan Shushud's *Masters of Wisdom of Central Asia,* trans. from the Turkish by Muhtar Holland (Coombe Springs Press, 1983), p. 143.

3. Thich Nhat Hanh, *The Heart of Understanding: Commentaries on the Heart Sutra* (Berkeley, CA: Parallax Press, 1988), p. 41.

A BRIEF ACCOUNT OF RUMI'S LIFE

4. Franklin D. Lewis, *Rumi: Past and Present, East and West* (Oxford, England: One World Publishers, 2000), p. 193.

CHAPTER 1. SPONTANEOUS WANDERING

*Introductory Note*

5. Panzaic: a made-up adjective for Sancho Panza, who rode a different journey than Quixote. He deserves his own quixotic word. No gaunt, bookish savior of damsels, the panzaic rider smells of donkey

and spilled beer. He's commonsensical, ambitious for himself and family, earthy, and very loyal in his friendship.

6. Pir Vilayat Khan: the son and designated successor of Hazrat Inayat Khan, educated at the Sorbonne and Oxford. During the Second World War he served as a pilot in the British Royal Navy. After the war Pir Vilayat continued his spiritual training by studying with masters of many different traditions throughout India and the Middle East. He is a Pir in the lineage of the Chisti Sufi order. While honoring the initiatic tradition, Pir Vilayat is continually pioneering updated practices in the evolution of consciousness.

7. pp. xi–xii, 76, Nanao Sakaki, *Break the Mirror,* Blackberry Books, 1996. Originally published by North Point Press, 1987. See also *Let's Eat Stars* and *Nanao or Never* from Blackberry Books, 617 E. Neck Rd., Nobleboro, ME 04555 or www.blackberrybooksinc.com.

*Five Things*

8. Rabia (d. 801): the woman mystic from Basra who said that a love for God should not come out of fear or hope but in response to the beauty in the heart. She once sat indoors with her eyes closed on a lovely spring morning to teach that external magnificence is only a reflection of inner kindness and generosity, and that is divine grace.

9. *Sema:* the deep listening of the ecstatic turning.

*The Many Wines*

10. Majnun is the lover who loses his reason in the overwhelming experience of love for Layla—a good start. In the fourth grade I wrote such an extravagantly mushy valentine to Sandra Martin that it caused our parents to talk seriously on the phone for a long time. That was the 1940s. I wonder what I wrote.

*Cooked Heads*

11. A *cooked head* has gone beyond mind and desire, beyond inner and outer, freed of time and space yet still *here,* and on the road to Tabriz as well.

## CHAPTER 2. *SOHBET*

*Introductory Note*

12. Am I not your lord?: The original agreement between the divine and the human is called *Alast.* It's a short conversation. God asks

in Arabic, *Alastu bi-rabbikum,* "Am I not your Lord?" Rumi hears this question addressed to the not-yet-created humanity as a music that starts human consciousness dancing the instant, simultaneous, reply of manifest being, YES!

13. The Emily Dickinson quote is from R. W. Franklin's edition of *The Poems of Emily Dickinson* (Cambridge: Harvard University Press, Belknap Press, 1998), no. 466.

14. Kenneth Rexroth, *Sacramental Acts,* ed. Sam Hamill and Elaine Laura Kleiner (Port Townsend, WA: Copper Canyon, 1997), p. 25.

*You Are Not Your Eyes*

15. *Illa* and *La* are parts of the *zikr,* the vocal or silent remembering, "There is no reality but God; there is only God." *La'illaha il'Allahu* is said to have three parts. The first part, *La'illaha,* is the denial, the abandonment of everything. The second part, *il'Allah,* the intrusion, the explosion into the individual of divine presence. *Hu,* the third part, is the out-breathing of that presence. Another way of saying what *zikr* is, is that *La'illaha* is the manifestation of creation and *il'Allahu,* the essence, that which created the cosmos. So the saying of it merges the two with in-breath and out-breath.

*Imra'u 'l-Qays*

16. Imra'u 'l-Qays (d. ca. A.D. 540) is considered the best pre-Islamic poet in Arabic. He is credited with being the first in that tradition to catch the reader's attention by referring at the beginning of a poem to a lost love.

## CHAPTER 3. THE SUPERABUNDANCE OF ORDINARY BEING

*Introductory Note*

17. Rainer Maria Rilke, *Ahead of All Parting,* trans. Stephen Mitchell (New York: Random House, 1995), p. 387.

*Zuleikha*

18. Zuleikha was the wife of Potiphar the Egyptian. For Rumi she is a type of the lover, like Majnun, so lost in her love for the handsome Joseph that she hears every phrase and every natural sound, the wind, the fire's crackling, birdcalls, as messages from Joseph.

## CHAPTER 4. SUDDEN WHOLENESS

*Introductory Note*

19. The first two haiku are from Basho, *On Love and Barley, Haiku of Basho,* trans. Lucien Stryk (New York: Penguin Books, 1985), pp. 72, 43. The last is from Robert Hass's *Essential Haiku* (Hopewll, NJ: Ecco, 1994), p. 11.

## CHAPTER 6. A NEW LIFE

*Introductory Note*

20. In dreams: I came across this Gilani reference in Andrew Harvey's *Perfume of the Desert* (Wheaton, IL: Quest Books, 1999), p. 55.

21. Bawa Muhaiyaddeen, *The Book of God's Love* (Philadelphia: Fellowship Press, 1981), p. 84.

*Nasuh's Changing*

22. For the full story of Nasuh see *The Essential Rumi,* pp. 161–65.

## CHAPTER 7. GRIEF

*Introductory Note*

23. "The feel of not to feel it" is from Keats's sonnet "In drear-nighted December . . ."

*The Death of Saladin*

24. Saladin: Saladin Zarkub, a goldsmith in Konya. There are hagiographic miniatures that show Rumi leading Saladin out of his goldsmith's shop and into the street to begin the *sema.* Rumi heard an essential music in the goldsmith's hammering and began to turn in the ecstasy of his listening. Saladin had come to Konya in 1235, already a student, like Rumi, of Burhan Maqaqqiq. When Shams arrived in 1244, the two would meet in Saladin's shop or in his home. After Shams's disappearance, Saladin became the friend that Rumi loved as a reminder of the deep presence. In 1248 when Saladin died, Rumi led a mystical dance with flute and drum through the streets of Konya to celebrate Saladin's *urs,* the soul union of a great being with the divine. The friendship of Saladin and Rumi was further strengthened by the marriage of Rumi's oldest son, Sultan Velad, to Saladin's daughter Fateme Khatun.

## CHAPTER 8. TAVERN MADNESS

*Introductory Note*

25. The Junnaiyd quotation is from Andrew Harvey's *Perfume of the Desert* (Wheaton, IL: Quest Books, 1999), p. 146.

26. The story of Buddha and Mara is from Thich Nhat Hanh's *The Heart of Understanding: Commentaries on the Heart Sutra* (Berkeley, CA: Parallax Press, 1988), pp. 42–45.

27. Matzoobs are crazy wisdom people, as irrational as a tiny mantis in our front yard, or Tibet, or a quantum leap through a black hole, or love, or an aneurysm in the brain, or dreams of the dead fixing food. Matzoobs know the mad health of Macchu Picchu and the statuette of a ram caught in a golden thicket that archeologists found in the graves of Ur.

## CHAPTER 9. ABSENCE

*Introductory Note*

28. Junnaiyd (d. 910) played a key role in establishing the "sober" school of Sufism.

29. *The Poems of Emily Dickinson* (Cambridge: Harvard University Press, Belknap Press, 1998), p. 517, no. 1344.

30. I reworked this quatrain from a version quoted in Andrew Harvey's *Perfume of the Desert*, p. xiii.

## CHAPTER 10. ANIMAL ENERGIES

*Introductory Note*

31. Hazrat Inayat Khan, founder of the Sufi Order International, came to the West in 1910 as representative of the highest musical traditions of India. He brought a message of love, harmony, and beauty that was the essence of Sufi teaching and a revolutionary approach to harmonizing Western and Eastern spirituality. He says, "The work of the inner life is to make God a reality, so that He is no more an imagination; that this relationship that man has with God may seem to him more real than any other relationship in this world; and when this happens, then all relationships, however near and dear, become less binding. But at the same time, a person does not become cold; he becomes more loving." From *The Inner Life, The Sufi Message of Hazrat Inayat Khan*, vol. 1 (The Hague: East-West Publications, 1989).

## CHAPTER 11. LOVE'S SECRET

*Introductory Note*

32. *The Glance* (New York: Viking, 1999), p. 34.

## CHAPTER 13. SHIFT FROM ROMANCE TO FRIENDSHIP

*The Wrist*

33. Muhammad's Night of Power, the night on which the Qur'an came through him, is traditionally celebrated on the twenty-seventh night of Ramadan.

## CHAPTER 14. UNION

*Introductory Note*

34. Bawa Muhaiyaddeen: I had thought to put here a brief biography, but I can't do it. As he taught so beautifully, a human being is too vast to be put in words. Bawa always turned away questions about his personal life. I am not the one to try to say who the being was who came to me in a dream in a ball of light on May 2, 1977. I am grateful beyond words for the heart-opening work he did and that continues with me.

## CHAPTER 15. DIE BEFORE YOU DIE

*Husam*

35. Husam: Husam Chelebi, Rumi's scribe, and one of Shams's students. One day Rumi and Husam were walking in the gardens of Meram. Husam suggested that Rumi begin a poem in the *masnavi* form (rhyming couplets), whereupon Rumi pulled from his turban the first eighteen lines of what was to become the opening of Book I of his masterwork, the *Masnavi,* the famous "Reed Flute's Song" section. During the next twelve years the mysterious collaboration continued. Rumi sometimes refers to the *Masnavi* as "The Book of Husam," and he often says that he is the empty flute, Husam the breath that makes the *Masnavi* music.

## CHAPTER 16. HARSH EVIDENCE

*Introductory Note*

36. W. H. Auden: The Auden stanza may be found in his *Collected* (Vintage), but more appropriately for the theme here, look for it in *Tell Me the Truth About Love, Ten Poems by W. H. Auden* (Random House), compiled in 1994 by Edward Mendelson, executor of Auden's estate. Here are the final three stanzas of "As I Walked Out One Evening."

"O look, look in the mirror,
O look in your distress;
Life remains a blessing
although you cannot bless.

"O stand, stand at the window
As the tears scald and start;
You shall love your crooked neighbour
With your crooked heart."

It was late, late in the evening,
The lovers they were gone;
The clocks had ceased their chiming,
And the deep river ran on.

*Kharraqani's Marriage*

37. Kharraqani (d. 1034) is one of those Sufis who have no visible teacher. "I am amazed at those who declare that they require this or that master. You are well aware that I have never been taught by any man. God was my guide, though I have the greatest respect for all the masters." Others in this "line" are Attar of Nishapur, who was guided by the being of light of Hallaj Mansour, and Ibn Arabi, who was a disciple of Khidr, the invisible master of those who are masterless! Khidr's "guidance" does not consist in leading all uniformly to the same goal. Khidr helps one attain to the Khidr of one's individual being, the spring of life, the esoteric truth that frees one from literal religion. Kharraqani says, "Each person is oriented toward a quest for his personal invisible guide, or he entrusts himself to the collective, magisterial authority as the intermediary between himself and revelation."

## CHAPTER 18. LOVE DOGS

*Love Dogs*

38. Khidr; another name for a mysterious, but nonetheless real, function. This one has to do with how we are guided in our inner lives by one beyond our knowing. Khidr in the Islamic world is felt to be a being that exists on the edge between the seen and unseen. When Moses vows to find the place "where the two seas meet," he encounters Khidr. There have been other sightings.

He is associated with the color green. Although not mentioned by name in the *Qur'an,* he is assumed to be the one that Moses meets and wishes to travel with and learn from, who does such violent and inexplicable things that Moses cannot bear to be with him. In the famous story (*Qur'an* 18:60–83) Moses and Khidr must part, after Khidr explains the reasons for what he has done, because Moses does not have patience enough to endure the truth of Khidr's harsh obedience.

Khidr seems especially connected with solitaries and those without visible teachers. Ibrahim, who gave up his kingdom for the kingdom within, says, "I lived four years in the wilderness. Khidr the Green Ancient was my companion. He taught me the Name of God."

## CHAPTER 19. ONE STROKE DOWN

*Introductory Note*

39. Al-Hallaj Mansour was martyred in Baghdad in 922 for saying, *Ana'l Haqq,* or *I am the truth. I am God.*

## CHAPTER 20. LOVE'S EXCESS

*Introductory Note*

40. Bawa Muhaiyaddeen, *A Mystical Journey* (Philadephia: Fellowship Press, 1990), p. 92.

41. In Discourse No. 10 Rumi tells a story of his father, Bahauddin. A government official comes to ask advice. Bahauddin says the official shouldn't have taken the chance. "I am subject to various states," he explains. "In one I can speak and in another I do not speak. In one state I can listen to the stories of other lives and respond to them. In another I withdraw to my room and see no one. In yet another I am utterly distraught, absorbed in God, unable to communicate at all. It's too risky for you to have come here on the chance I might be able to have conversation." In his surrender, these regions flow over him like weather.

He's not in control of them. He's on retreat with his outrageous soul. This is the fluidity and freedom of love's excess.

## CHAPTER 22. LORD OF THE HEART

*Introductory Note*

42. This Ruskin quote is from *Modern Painters,* vol.3, pt. 4, ch. 16.

43. *Questions of Life—Answers of Wisdom,* vol. 2 (Philadelphia: Fellowhip Press, 2001), pp. 40–41.

## A NOTE ON TRANSLATION

The Monotones from Newark, New Jersey—lead singer Charles Patrick, with Warren Davis, George Malone, Warren and John Ryanes, and John Smith—are the quintessential one-hit wonders of the 1950s. These five young men hit upon the words and music of "The Book of Love," and while they were rehearsing, some children outside were throwing a ball against the wall. At a key point the ball hit the window, not breaking it but making a loud BOOM, right at the point where that now appears in the song. Everyone agreed it should be incorporated.

Well I wonder, wonder whom, de doo doo, who
*BOOM* (the children's ball)
who wrote the book of love . . .

I like the grammatical wavering between *whom* and the more natural who. Sufis hear that sound as the breathing creative vibration, Huuuuuu. Boom.

# *Index of Titles and First Lines*

# Credits

Grateful acknowledgement is made to the following for permission to reprint previously published material.

W. H. Auden: "As I Walked Out One Evening," copyright © 1940 and renewed 1968 by W. H. Auden., from *W. H. Auden: The Collected Poems* by W. H. Auden. Used by permission of Random House, Inc.

Rainer Maria Rilke: "Elegy 9," from *The Selected Poetry of Rainer Maria Rilke,* translated by Stephen Mitchell, copyright © 1982 by Stephen Mitchell. Used by permission of Random House, Inc.

Basho: "Even in Kyoto," *The Essential Haiku: Versions of Basho, Busson & Issa, Edited and with an Introduction by Robert Hass.* Introduction and selection copyright © 1994 by Robert Hass. Used by permission of HarperCollins Publishers. "Samurai talk" and "You, the butterfly," from *On Love and Barley* by Basho, translated by Lucien Stryk, copyright © 1985 by Lucien Stryk. Used by permission of Penguin Publishers.

Rumi: Poems originally published in *Open Secret, Unseen Rain, This Longing,* and *Feeling the Shoulder of the Lion,* translated by John Moyne and Coleman Barks. Introductions and translations copyright © 1984, 1986, 1988, 1991 by Coleman Barks. Reprinted by arrangement with Shambhala Publications, Inc., Boston, www.shambhala.com.

Emily Dickinson: #466 "I dwell in possibility," and #1344 "The infinite a sudden guest," reprinted by permission of the publishers and the Trustees of Amherst College from *The Poems of Emily Dickinson: Variorum Edition,* Ralph W. Franklin, ed., Cambridge, MS.: The Belknap Press of Harvard University Press, copyright © 1998 by the President and Fellows of Harvard College. Copyright © 1951, 1955, 1979 by the President and Fellows of Harvard College.

Nanao and Gary Snyder: Nanao's poem "Go with Muddy Feet," and Snyder's comments are reprinted by permission of Blackberry Books, 617 East Neck Road, Nobleboro, ME 04555. www.blackberrybooksme.com.

Kenneth Rexroth: 9 lines from "When We With Sappho," from *Collected Shorter Poems,* copyright © 1944 by Kenneth Rexroth. Reprinted by permission of New Directions Publishing Corp.

Thich Nhat Hanh: Reprinted from *The Heart of Understanding: Commentaries on the Prajnaparamita Heart Sutra* (1988) by Thich Nhat Hanh with permission of Parallax Press, Berkeley, CA, www.parallax.org.